Level 6 Maths

Pupil Book

Rachel Axten-Higgs

Loop Step 49463T COLLINS PRIMARY FOCUS MATHS - LEVEL 6 MATHS PUPIL BOOK - ad.UK.aip.01

William Collins' dream of knowledge for all began with the publication of his first book in 1819. A self-educated mill worker, he not only enriched millions of lives, but also founded a flourishing publishing house. Today, staying true to this spirit, Collins books are packed with inspiration, innovation and practical expertise. They place you at the centre of a world of possibility and give you exactly what you need to explore it.

Collins. Freedom to teach.

Published by Collins

An imprint of HarperCollins*Publishers*
77–85 Fulham Palace Road
Hammersmith
London
W6 8JB

Browse the complete Collins catalogue at
www.collins.co.uk

© HarperCollins*Publishers* Limited 2013

10 9 8 7 6 5 4 3 2 1

ISBN-978-0-00-753116-5

Rachel Axten-Higgs asserts her moral rights to be identified as the author of this work

British Library Cataloguing in Publication Data
A Catalogue record for this publication is available from the British Library

Edited by Marie Taylor and Lynn Thomson
Cover design by Neil Adams
Cover artwork by Steve Evans
Internal design by Neil Adams
Illustrations by Steve Evans and Jouve
Typeset by Jouve

Printed and bound by L.E.G.O. S.p.A. Italy

Contents

Progression maps

Number

LEVEL 5

LEVEL 6

Level 5	Level 6
Use equivalence between fractions	→ Calculate fractions of quantities (fraction answers)
Understand simple ratio	→ Divide a quantity into two or more parts in a given ratio
Order fractions and decimals	→ Use the equivalence of fractions, decimals and percentages to compare proportions
Solve simple problems involving ratio and direct proportion	→ Solve problems involving direct proportion
Reduce a fraction to its simplest form by cancelling common factors	→ Add and subtract fractions by writing them with a common denominator
	→ Multiply and divide an integer by a fraction
Use a calculator where appropriate to calculate fractions/percentages of quantities/measurements	→ Calculate percentages and find the outcome of a given percentage increase and decrease
	→ Use proportional reasoning to solve a problem, choosing the correct number to take as 100%, or a whole

Algebra

LEVEL

Construct, express in symbolic form and use simple formulae involving one or two operations

Use systematic trial and improvement methods to find approximate solutions to equations such as $x^3 + x = 20$

Construct and solve linear equations with integer coefficients, using an appropriate method

Generate terms of a sequence using term-to-term and position-to-term definitions

Write an expression for the nth term of an arithmetic sequence

Use and interpret coordinates in all four quadrants

Plot the graph of linear functions, where y is given explicitly in terms of x

Recognise that equations of the form $y = mx + c$ correspond to straight-line graphs

Interpret graphs arising from real-life situations

Construct functions arising from real-life problems and plot their graphs

Shape, space and measure

LEVEL 5

LEVEL 6

Use a range of properties of 2D and 3D shapes and identify all the symmetries of 2D shapes

→ **Classify quadrilaterals by their geometric properties**

→ **Use 2D representations of 3D objects**

→ **Identify alternate and corresponding angles and understand proofs of the angle sum of a triangle and a quadrilateral**

Know and use the angle sum of a triangle and of angles at a point

→ **Use the properties of angles, of parallel and intersecting lines, and of triangles and other polygons**

Reason about position and movement and transform shapes

→ **Enlarge 2D shapes given a centre of enlargement and a positive whole number scale factor**

→ **Know that translations, rotations and reflections preserve length and angle and map objects onto congruent images**

Measure and draw angles to the nearest degree

→ **Use straight edge and compasses**

Use the formula for the area of a rectangle

→ **Deduce and use the formulae for the area of a triangle and a parallelogram**

Distinguish area from perimeter

→ **Calculate volumes and surface areas of cuboids**

→ **Know and use the formulae for the circumference and area of a circle**

Handling data

LEVEL 5

LEVEL 6

Plan how to collect data to answer questions

→ Design a survey or experiment

→ Construct tables for sets of raw data

Interpret graphs and diagrams, including pie charts, and draw conclusions

→ Select and construct pie charts for categorical data

→ Select and construct bar charts and frequency diagrams for discrete and continuous data

→ Communicate interpretations and results of a survey using selected tables, graphs and diagrams in support

Create and interpret line graphs

→ Select and construct simple time graphs for time series

→ Select and construct scatter graphs

Find probabilities based on equally likely outcomes or experimental evidence

→ Find and record all possible mutually exclusive outcomes for single events and two successive events in a systematic way

Understand and use the probability scale from 0 to 1

→ Know and use the fact that the sum of probabilities of all mutually exclusive outcomes is 1

Number

Fractions of quantities

LEVEL 5

LEVEL 6

| **Vocabulary** | equivalent; fraction; quantity |

Getting started

Use equivalence between fractions

- Two fractions are equivalent when they have the same value.
- For example, $\frac{2}{8}$ is equivalent to $\frac{1}{4}$ since $\frac{2 \div 2}{8 \div 2} = \frac{1}{4}$
- It is important to be able to find the equivalence between fractions so you can solve problems involving fractions with different denominators.

1. Find three equivalent fractions for each of these:

   a) $\frac{1}{2}$ b) $\frac{1}{4}$ c) $\frac{1}{10}$

2. Find three equivalent fractions for each of these:

   a) $\frac{92}{100}$ b) $\frac{4}{5}$ c) $\frac{19}{21}$

Next steps

Calculate fractions of quantities (fraction answers)

- If you are asked to find what 225 g is as a fraction of 750 g, work through it like this:

  Write as a fraction: $\dfrac{\text{amount to find}}{\text{total amount}} = \dfrac{225}{750}$

  Simplify the fraction by dividing the numerator and the denominator by common factors: $\dfrac{225 \div 25}{750 \div 25} = \dfrac{9}{30}$

  $\dfrac{9 \div 3}{30 \div 10} = \dfrac{3}{10}$

  3 is a prime number, so we know this is in its lowest terms.

  So, 225 g as a fraction of 750 g is $\frac{3}{10}$.

◯ Remember

To find an equivalent fraction, do the same to the numerator and the denominator (e.g. multiply both by 2).

3. 9900 people watched a netball game. Of these, 7200 were female.

   a) What fraction of the spectators were female?

   b) What fraction of the spectators were male?

4. In a school with 540 people, $\frac{1}{9}$ were men, $\frac{1}{3}$ were women and the rest were children. What fraction were children?

5. 30 500 people live in Westborough City. Of these, 9500 are adult females, 11 500 are children and the rest are adult males.

   a) What fraction of the city are adult females?

   b) What fraction of the city are children?

   c) What fraction of the city are adult males?

6. The total number of marks for a mathematics test is 95. Thomas scored 90, Zack scored 75 and Lizzie scored 68. Express each child's mark as a fraction in its lowest terms.

7. The total cost of a house renovation was £56 800. The materials cost £45 000 and the labour costs were £11 800.

   a) Express the cost of the materials as a fraction of the total cost of the renovation. Give your answer in its lowest terms.

   b) What fraction of the total cost was the labour? Give your answer in its lowest terms.

8. The total prize money for a spelling competition was £567.

   Half of this total was awarded for the first prize.

   The third prize was £56.70.

   The rest of the money was for the second prize.

   a) How much was the first prize?

   b) What fraction of the prize money was the third prize?

   c) How much was the second prize?

   d) What fraction of the prize money was the second prize?

Comparing proportions

> **Vocabulary**   ordering; fractions; decimals; equivalence; percentages; proportion

Getting started

Order fractions and decimals

- To order fractions, convert them to equivalent fractions with common denominators.

- The **lowest** common denominator can be one of the denominators that is already used.

- For example, to order $\frac{1}{2}, \frac{2}{8}, \frac{5}{16}, \frac{3}{4}$:

  Find the common denominator: 16

  Find the equivalent fractions:

  $$\frac{1 \times 8}{2 \times 8} = \frac{8}{16}, \frac{2 \times 2}{8 \times 2} = \frac{4}{16}, \frac{3 \times 4}{4 \times 4} = \frac{12}{16}$$

  Order the fractions: $\frac{4}{16}, \frac{5}{16}, \frac{8}{16}, \frac{12}{16}$

  Put them back to their original form to answer the question: $\frac{2}{8}, \frac{5}{16}, \frac{1}{2}, \frac{3}{4}$

1. Order the following decimals from **smallest** to **largest**.

   a) 16·75, 16·71, 16·7001, 16·84, 15·95

   b) 39·01, 39·001, 39·1, 39·005, 39·05

   c) 6·12, 6·21, 6·012, 6·22, 6·56

2. Order the following fractions from **largest** to **smallest**.

   a) $\frac{1}{2}, \frac{14}{16}, \frac{3}{4}, \frac{5}{8}$

   b) $\frac{14}{25}, \frac{1}{2}, \frac{1}{5}, \frac{6}{10}$

   c) $\frac{1}{3}, \frac{7}{9}, \frac{25}{27}, \frac{4}{9}$

Next steps

Use the equivalence of fractions, decimals and percentages to compare proportions

- If you are given a range of quantities in different formats to compare, e.g. fractions, decimals and percentages, convert them to a common format first and then compare them.

- For example, to compare $\frac{1}{2}$, 0·6, 0·3 and 88%:

Convert to percentages: 50%, 60%, 30% and 88%

Then compare or order them.

◯ Remember

Put fractions or decimals back to their original form when you write them in order. Always check whether you need to write them from largest to smallest or smallest to largest.

3. Write these percentages as fractions and simplify them as far as possible.

   a) 58%

   b) 123%

   c) 19%

   d) 225%

4. Write these decimals as percentages.

   a) 0·9

   b) 0·43

   c) 0·234

   d) 3·75

5. Write these fractions as percentages. Round your answers to 1 decimal place if necessary.

   a) $\frac{3}{8}$

   b) $\frac{5}{13}$

   c) $\frac{17}{21}$

   d) $\frac{63}{85}$

6. Is $\frac{6}{12}$ half of $\frac{12}{24}$? State **yes** or **no** and explain, mathematically, how you know.

> **Vocabulary**   ratio; quantity; division; fraction; ratio notation; comparative

⑤ LEVEL

Getting started

Understand simple ratio

- Ratio is the comparative value of two or more amounts. It can be written as numbers separated by colons, e.g. 3 : 4, or as a fraction.

- You can simplify ratios by using common factors.

- For example, 8 : 4 = 4 : 2 (both parts can divide by 2).

1. Look at the coloured strip below.

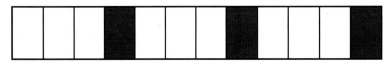

    a)   Write the ratio of white to red squares.

    b)   Write the ratio of red to white squares.

2. In a bag of counters there are 16 blue counters and 28 yellow counters. Write the ratio of yellow to blue counters as simply as possible.

⑥ LEVEL

Next steps

Divide a quantity into two or more parts in a given ratio

- If you are given a ratio and told one of the quantities, you can work out the other quantity or quantities and the total amount.

- For example, if the ratio of boys to girls in a class is 3 : 2 and there are 18 boys, use division to find out how many girls there are:

(18 ÷ 3) × 2 = 6 × 2 = 12 girls

Add the number of boys to girls to find the total:

18 + 12 = 30 children in the class

Remember

Always check that you have written the ratio in the correct order, for example red to blue, or blue to red.

3. Some children did a traffic survey outside their school and found that during the morning rush hour 165 cars and buses passed by. The ratio of cars to buses was 9 : 2. How many cars passed by?

4. A new colour of paint is made by mixing 3 parts blue with 4 parts red. 665 ml of the new paint is mixed. How much of this is blue paint?

5. A recipe for a sponge cake uses flour and sugar in the ratio 3 : 2. How much sugar is needed if 270 g of flour is used?

6. On a visit to a museum, the children are split into three groups in the ratio 6 : 8 : 4. There are 108 children in total. How many are there in each group?

7. A fruit salad contains 5 different fruits. They are in the ratio of 6 : 3 : 2 : 3 : 4 being strawberries : peaches : apples : raspberries : grapes. If there are 52 g of grapes, find the number of grams of each of the other fruits.

8. Chris, Sandeep and Ana all collect money for the same charity. Between them, they collect £88. The ratio of the money they collected is 1 : 4 : 3. How much did each person collect?

⑤ Getting started

Solve simple problems involving ratio and direct proportion

- Direct proportion means a direct relationship between two quantities: when one quantity increases or decreases, the other quantity also increases or decreases in the same ratio.

- For example, concentrated squash is mixed with water in the ratio 1 : 9. This means that there is nine times as much water as there is squash. If there is 100 ml of squash, there will be 900 ml of water. 1 : 9, 100 : 900 and 2 : 18 are all equivalent ratios.

1. One cake serves six people.

   a) Write this as a ratio.

   b) Write an equivalent ratio showing the number of people that 4 cakes serve.

   c) Write an equivalent ratio showing the number of people that 72 cakes serve.

2. A bag of marbles contains 8 large marbles, 24 medium marbles and 30 small marbles.

   a) Write the ratio of large marbles : medium marbles : small marbles in the bag.

   b) An identical bag of marbles is tipped in to the first bag of marbles. Write an equivalent ratio showing the new quantities in the bag.

   c) The marbles added in part (b) are removed. Half of each type of marble is then taken out of the bag. Write an equivalent ratio showing the new quantities in the bag.

⑥ Next steps

Solve problems involving direct proportion

- When a question involves direct proportion, all parts of the ratio increase or decrease in the same way.

- For example, if a recipe for 8 people says 300g of pasta, 140g cheese, 200g tomatoes and 350g of vegetables, the quantities are in the ratio:

  300 : 140 : 200 : 350

  If the recipe is altered to serve 4 people, each quantity in the ratio is halved, because 4 is half of 8.

  The new quantities are therefore: 150 : 70 : 100 : 175

> ## 🔍 Remember
> Find equivalent ratios by multiplying or dividing both parts by the same number.

3. A recipe for soup to serve 6 people is: 100g carrots, 50g coriander, 200g stock and 150g potatoes.

   a) Write these quantities as a ratio.

   b) How much of each ingredient is needed to serve 2 people?

   c) Write the quantities to serve 8 people as a ratio.

4. Delia is making a traybake. She uses the following ingredients for one bowl of traybake mixture.

   4 cups plain flour

   3 cups sugar

   $\frac{1}{2}$ cup baking powder

   2 cups chocolate

   1·5 cups butter

   a) If she has one cup of plain flour, how many bowls of traybake mixture can she make?

   b) If she has one cup of chocolate, how many bowls of traybake mixture can she make?

5. Look at the following information about **Shakira** and **Rebecca**.

   Shakira was born in **1998**.

   Rebecca was born in **2010**.

   They have the same birthday.

   The ratio of **Shakira's** age to **Rebecca's** age on their birthday in **2011** was **13 : 1**.

   a) What was the ratio of Shakira's age to Rebecca's age on their birthday in 2014? Write the ratio in its simplest form.

   b) In what year will the ratio of Shakira's age to Rebecca's be age 3 : 2?

6. A duckling lived in a cage. It doubled in size every day. After 16 days it filled the cage and had to be moved to another cage. After how many days did the duckling half-fill the cage?

Adding and subtracting fractions

> **Vocabulary** addition; subtraction; fraction; factor; common factor; simplest form

Getting started

Reduce a fraction to its simplest form by cancelling common factors

- Common factors of fractions are factors that are the same in the numerator and the denominator of a fraction.
- Use common prime factors to cancel fractions to their simplest form.
- For example, $\frac{12}{18}$

  12 as a product of prime factors: $2 \times 2 \times 3$

  18 as a product of prime factors: $2 \times 3 \times 3$

  Cancel the numerator and denominator by common prime factors: $2 \times 3 = 6$

  $$\frac{\cancel{12}^{\,2}}{\cancel{18}_{\,3}} = \frac{2}{3}$$

1. Find the prime factors of these numbers.

   a) 56   b) 16

   c) 22   d) 34

2. Write these fractions in their simplest terms by finding and cancelling common prime factors.

   a) $\frac{12}{16}$ b) $\frac{24}{30}$

   c) $\frac{20}{50}$ d) $\frac{13}{24}$

Next steps

Add and subtract fractions by writing them with a common denominator

- Fractions must have the same denominator before you can add or subtract them.
- Find the lowest common denominator, convert the fractions and the calculation is straightforward.

- For example, $\frac{4}{5} - \frac{3}{10}$

  Lowest common denominator = 10

  So, $\frac{4}{5} - \frac{3}{10} = \frac{8}{10} - \frac{3}{10} = \frac{5}{10} = \frac{1}{2}$

- For example, $\frac{3}{9} + \frac{2}{6}$

  Lowest common denominator = 18

  So, $\frac{3}{9} + \frac{2}{6} = \frac{6}{18} + \frac{6}{18} = \frac{12}{18} = \frac{2}{3}$

◯ Remember

Prime factors are prime numbers that multiply together to make a number.

3. Add these fractions. Give your answers as mixed numbers.

   a) $\frac{5}{9} + \frac{2}{3}$

   b) $\frac{4}{7} + \frac{1}{2}$

   c) $\frac{5}{6} + \frac{8}{12}$

   d) $\frac{3}{4} + \frac{10}{16}$

4. Complete these subtractions. Give your answers as proper fractions or mixed numbers.

   a) $\frac{5}{8} - \frac{3}{6}$

   b) $4\frac{1}{2} - \frac{9}{12}$

   c) $1\frac{3}{8} - \frac{5}{6}$

   d) $\frac{13}{25} - \frac{2}{5}$

5. Jacob took part in two races. In the first race he ran $3\frac{4}{5}$ laps of the playing field. In the second race he ran $5\frac{5}{6}$ laps of the playing field. How many laps of the playing field did he run altogether?

6. Barbara read $\frac{2}{12}$ of her book before school, $\frac{2}{6}$ of her book at school and another $\frac{3}{18}$ before bed.

   a) How much did she read altogether?

   b) How much does she have left to read?

7. $\frac{1}{8} + \frac{3}{4} = \frac{4}{12}$

   What is wrong with this? Explain your answer fully and write the correct answer to the calculation.

8. $\frac{16}{25} - \frac{3}{5} = \frac{13}{20}$

   What is wrong with this? Explain your answer fully and write the correct answer to the calculation.

Multiplying and dividing integers by fractions

> **Vocabulary**   multiplication; division; fraction; integer; common factor; simplest form

Getting started

Reduce a fraction to its simplest form by cancelling common factors

- Common factors of fractions are factors that are the same in the numerator and the denominator of a fraction.
- Use common prime factors to cancel fractions to their simplest form.
- For example, $\frac{8}{12}$

  8 written as a product of prime factors: $2 \times 2 \times 2$

  12 written as a product of prime factors: $2 \times 2 \times 3$

  Cancel the numerator and denominator by common prime factors: $2 \times 2 = 4$

  $$\frac{\overset{2}{\cancel{8}}}{\underset{3}{\cancel{12}}} = \frac{2}{3}$$

1. Find the prime factors of these numbers.

   a) 18   b) 21

   c) 32   d) 45

2. Write the following fractions in their simplest terms by finding and cancelling common prime factors.

   a) $\frac{20}{25}$ b) $\frac{18}{21}$

   c) $\frac{18}{32}$ d) $\frac{21}{45}$

Next steps

Multiply and divide an integer by a fraction

- Multiplying or dividing an integer by a fraction is the same as multiplying or dividing two fractions. This is because the integer can be expressed as a fraction with a denominator of 1.

- For example, $7 \times \frac{4}{5}$ can be written as $\frac{7}{1} \times \frac{4}{5}$.

To multiply fractions, multiply the two numerators together and the two denominators together: $\frac{7 \times 4}{1 \times 5} = \frac{28}{5}$

This is an improper fraction that can then be expressed as a mixed number: $5\frac{5}{3}$

- For example, $9 \div \frac{3}{8}$ can be written as $\frac{9}{1} \div \frac{3}{8}$

To divide fractions, switch the numerator and denominator of the second fraction and then multiply them: $\frac{9}{1} \times \frac{8}{3} = \frac{9 \times 8}{1 \times 3} = \frac{72}{3}$

This is an improper fraction that can then be expressed as a whole number: 24

Remember

Prime factors that appear in the numerator and denominator can be cancelled.

---

3. Complete the following calculations. Give your answers as improper numbers or mixed numbers.

a) $9 \times \frac{4}{7}$

b) $6 \times \frac{3}{18}$

c) $8 \times \frac{12}{16}$

d) $5 \times \frac{3}{5}$

e) $11 \times \frac{5}{7}$

f) $121 \times \frac{1}{16}$

4. Complete the following calculations. Give your answers as improper numbers or mixed numbers.

a) $10 \div \frac{3}{8}$

b) $7 \div \frac{4}{9}$

c) $5 \div \frac{2}{16}$

d) $8 \div \frac{9}{12}$

e) $15 \div \frac{6}{9}$

f) $56 \div \frac{3}{7}$

5. A baker made 24 rolls. He then had a telephone order and made $\frac{4}{9}$ more rolls. How many rolls did he make altogether?

Calculating percentages

> **Vocabulary** percentages; calculate; percentage decrease; percentage increase

Getting started

LEVEL 5

Use a calculator where appropriate to calculate fractions / percentages of quantities / measurements

- 'Per cent' means 'out of 100'. Because the metric system of measures is based on 10, 100 and 1000, it is quite straightforward to find percentages of these.

- You can use a calculator to find harder percentages.

- For example, to find 23% of 4589 ml

  Enter:

  4 5 8 9 ÷ 1 0 0 =

  gives 1% = 45·89

  So **4 5 · 8 9 × 2 3 =** 1055·47 ml gives 23%.

- For example, if you are told that 14% of your earnings is £178.50 and need to find your total earnings:

  1 7 8 · 5 0 ÷ 1 4 =

  gives 1% = £12.75

  So **1 2 · 7 5 × 1 0 0 =** £1275 gives 100% of your earnings.

1. Use a calculator to find these amounts:

   a) 33% of 567 g

   b) 92% of 80 ml

   c) 7% of 635

   d) 28% of 234·50

2. Use a calculator to find these amounts:

   a) The total amount if £1306 is 24%

   b) The total amount if 567 g is 67%

   c) 67% of an amount if 9% is £567

   d) The total amount if 88% is 23 450

Calculate percentages and find the outcome of a given percentage increase and decrease

- To find a percentage increase or decrease, you may need to add or subtract the percentage you calculate from the original amount.

- For example, an item costing £50 is given a price increase of 15%. To find the new cost:

  First find the price increase of 15%: 50 ÷ 100 gives 1% = 0.5 (50p)

  50p × 15 = £7.50 gives 15%

  Add the original cost and the price increase to get the new cost of the item: £50 + £7.50 = £57.50

⚲ Remember

Find 1% of the total and multiply by 100 to find the total amount.

Give money answers in pounds to 2 decimal places and in pennies to the nearest whole number.

3. A shopkeeper decided to decrease all of his prices by 12% in order to attract more customers. The table shows the cost of the items before the decrease.

Item	Amount before decrease
Trousers	£34.50
Jumper	£28.99
Coat	£103.00
Socks	£4.89
Trainers	£57.98

a) Work out the amount of the decrease for each item.

b) Work out the new price of each item.

4. A toyshop had a sale. Before the sale, a playtent cost £67.99. During the sale, the same playtent cost £53.03. Find the percentage decrease of the playtent to the nearest one per cent.

5. In 2013, 56 children attended a safety event. This number increased to 1320 in 2014. Find the percentage increase from 2013 to 2014 to the nearest one per cent.

6. The original cost of an item is £80. In a sale, the same item costs £45. What is the percentage reduction?

Vocabulary	proportional reasoning; one hundred per cent; calculator; whole

LEVEL 5

Getting started

Use a calculator where appropriate to calculate fractions / percentages of quantities / measurements

- You can use a calculator to find fractions and percentages of amounts.

- To find a fraction of a quantity, divide the total amount by the denominator and multiply this number by the numerator. For example, to find $\frac{3}{5}$ of 960 g

Enter:

9 6 0 ÷ 5 =

This gives $\frac{1}{5}$ = 192

So **1 9 2 × 3 =** 576 g gives $\frac{3}{5}$

- For example, if you are told that 65% of your winnings is £2346 and want to know what 100% of your winnings would be:

2 3 4 6 ÷ 6 5 =

This gives 1% = £36.09

So **3 6 · 0 9 × 1 0 0 =** £3609.23 gives you 100% of your winnings.

1. Use a calculator to work out the following amounts:

   a) 61% of 888 g

   b) 11% of 103 ml

   c) 54% of 1587

   d) 34% of 589

2. Use a calculator to find the following fractions of the amounts shown:

   a) $\frac{7}{9}$ of 705   b) $\frac{6}{8}$ of 902·54

   c) $\frac{7}{21}$ of 888   d) $\frac{12}{20}$ of £187.50

Next steps

Use proportional reasoning to solve a problem, choosing the correct number to take as 100%, or a whole

- Proportional reasoning means using the concept of proportions (e.g. a ratio) to solve a mathematical problem (See Unit 4).

- To solve these problems and find a percentage increase or decrease, you need to identify which figure represents 100% first.

- For example, in this question:

There are 30 children in a class. $\frac{4}{6}$ of them are boys. How many girls are there in the class?

30 = 100% or one whole

$\frac{4}{6}$ are boys, so $1 - \frac{4}{6} = \frac{2}{6}$ must be girls.

$30 \div 6 = 5$

$5 \times 2 = 10$, so there are 10 girls in the class.

○ Remember

Using a calculator to work out percentages and fractions of amounts will save you a lot of time.

---

3. The results of a science experiment involving the distance a ball travelled down different heights of a slope are shown below:

Height of slope	Distance ball travelled
30 cm	2.56 m
50 cm	5.67 m
70 cm	8.94 m

  a) What is the overall percentage increase from 30 cm to 70 cm?

  b) What is the percentage increase from 50 cm to 70 cm?

4. A clothing shop had a sale where it took 12% off all of its stock. In the sale, Tim bought a board game for £4.56. How much was the board game before the sale?

5. A new floor cleaner usually costs £119.99. It is on sale at £89.99. What is the percentage reduction from the usual price to the sale price?

6. In a car showroom, a new model of car is being advertised at a cost of £9867. Customers can take the car away on a finance plan once they pay a deposit of 8%. What is the cost of the deposit?

Review

1. Nine students share a house. They pay £1335 per month rent which they share equally between them. Six of the students are male.

    a) What fraction of the rent does each student pay?

    b) What fraction of the rent is paid by the males? Give your answer in its simplest form.

    c) How much rent does each student pay?

    d) What is the total amount of rent paid by the females?

2. A recipe for butterfly cakes uses flour, butter and sugar in the ratio 4 : 3 : 6.

    a) If I make the cakes using 225 g of butter, how much flour and sugar should I use?

    b) If I use 100 g of flour, I can make 12 cakes. How much of each ingredient do I need to make 48 cakes?

3. A shopkeeper decides to hold a sale and reduce each of his sale items by a different amount. Copy and complete the table to show the amount and percentage reduction for each item.

Item	Amount before sale	Percentage decrease	Amount after sale
Chair	£65.00	13%	
Table	£179.00	20%	
Bed	£378.50		£344.43
Shelves	£85.75		£46.86

4. You are given this information:

    • On average, each person pays 70 pence per kg for potatoes in a supermarket.

    • On average, each person eats 55 kilograms of potatoes each year.

- The potato growers receive 18% of the money from the sale of potatoes.

How much of the money that each person pays for potatoes in one year goes to the **growers**?

5. Tamzin did three sponsored swims. In her first swim she swam $8\frac{1}{2}$ lengths of the pool. In her second swim she swam $4\frac{2}{3}$ lengths of the pool. In her final swim, she swam $12\frac{5}{6}$ lengths of the pool. How many lengths of the pool did she swim in total?

6. Complete these calculations. Show your working.

   a) $7 \times \dfrac{6}{8}$

   b) $13 \times \dfrac{5}{12}$

   c) $4 \times \dfrac{16}{21}$

   d) $20 \div \dfrac{4}{8}$

   e) $15 \div \dfrac{3}{8}$

   f) $8 \div \dfrac{3}{7}$

7. In 2013 there were 1345 children at a Furze Town secondary school. In 2014 the secondary school in a local village closed and the number of children at Furze Town increased by 12%.

   a) How many children joined Furze Town school?

   b) What was the total number of children at Furze Town school after the increase?

8. A clothing shop has a sale. Before the sale a coat cost £112.99. In the sale, the price was reduced by 15%.

   a) What was the amount of the percentage decrease?

   b) What was the sale price of the coat?

9. 456 children attend a music event.

   $\frac{3}{8}$ of them are girls.

   $\frac{5}{9}$ of the children play a woodwind instrument.

   a) What is the total number of girls?

   b) What is the total number of boys?

   c) How many of the children play a woodwind instrument?

Algebra

Systematic trial and improvement

Vocabulary	systematic; trial and improvement; equations; formulae; operations

Getting started

LEVEL 5

Construct, express in symbolic form and use simple formulae involving one or two operations

- $7(4r + 2)$ is an expression. If you are told the value of r, you can replace the letter r with a 3 to find the value of the expression, i.e. $7(4 \times 3 + 2) = 98$.

- $5w + 4 = 19$ is an equation. You can find the value of w, because $(5 \times 3 + 4) = 19$, so $w = 3$.

1. If $s = 7$, find the exact value of these expressions.

   a) $s(s + 8)$ b) $7s + 9$

   c) $12s - 13$ d) $4s(5s - 12 \cdot 5)$

2. Work out the value of the letter in each of these equations.

   a) $s + 7 = 15$ b) $3y = 12$

   c) $2w + 2 = 12$ d) $5t - 3 = 17$

Next steps

LEVEL 6

Use systematic trial and improvement methods to find approximate solutions to equations such as $x^3 + x = 20$

- Trial and improvement can be used to solve equations when you can't do it by a normal algebraic method. This is usually when a term in the equation is squared or cubed and the answer is often not a whole number.

- Drawing a table will help you be systematic when using trial and improvement. Decide on a number that you will replace the letter with and record how close your answer is to the actual answer. Use this information to decide whether the next number you try should be bigger or smaller.

- For example, to find the value of s in the equation $4s + s^2 = 15$:

s	$4s + s^2$	Comment
2	$8 + 4 = 12$	Too small
3	$12 + 9 = 21$	Too big
2·5	$10 + 6·25 = 16·25$	A little too big

Continue until you have found the answer that you need.

◯ Remember

Don't be scared of letters: they are simply replacing numbers. You can work out what the letters stand for by doing the calculations as if they were numbers, using trial and improvement or moving the letters to one side and numbers to the other.

3. Use systematic trial and improvement to work out the value of y in the equation $8y + y^3 = 1824$.

4. Use systematic trial and improvement to work out the value of g in the equation $16g - g^2 = 21·75$.

5. $7h + h^3 = 80$

   Create a table and use trial and improvement to find the value of h to 2 decimal places.

6. Use systematic trial and improvement to solve the equation $h(5h + 4) = 12·81$ (2 decimal places).

7. Zara has been trying to find the approximate solution to $k^3 + 5k = 34$.

Draw the table in your book and fill in the missing values. Continue the table until you find the approximate value of k.

k	$k^3 + 5k =$	Comment
3		Too big
2	$8 + 10 = 18$	
2·7		Just too small

8. A number multiplied by eight and then added to its square equals 153.

   a) Write an equation to show this using n for the number.

   b) Solve the equation using trial and improvement.

Constructing and solving linear equations

LEVEL 5

Getting started

Construct, express in symbolic form and use simple formulae involving one or two operations

- A formula is a rule that states the relationship between two or more variables. It can be written using letters and numbers.

- You can use a formula to find the value of one term if you know the value of the other variables in the formula.

- For example, $a = l \times w$ and $y = 2x + 4$ are both formulae.

  When $x = 2$, $y = 2x + 4 = (2 \times 2) + 4 = 8$.

1. If $x = 2{\cdot}5$, find the value of y in these formulae.

   a) $y = 2x$

   b) $3x + 8 = y$

   c) $y = 2(x + 7)$

   d) $8x - 4 = y$

   e) $y = 3x + (7x - 4)$

2. If $y = 2{\cdot}25$, work out the value of x in these formulae.

   a) $x = 3y$

   b) $2x = 6y$

   c) $8y - 4 = x$

   d) $12y + 8 = 7x$

LEVEL 6

Next steps

Construct and solve linear equations with integer coefficients, using an appropriate method

- A linear equation does not have any square or cube terms. For example, $y = 4x - 3$ and $7d - 8 = 45$ are both linear equations.

- To solve a linear equation, you can use inverse operations to move the numbers to one side and the letter terms to the other.

- For example, to solve $7d - 8 = 45$:

  Add 8 to each side (since $+8$ is the inverse of -8): $7d = 45 + 8$

  $$7d = 53$$

  Divide each side by 7 (since $\div 7$ is the inverse of $\times 7$): $d = 53 \div 7$

  $d = 7.57$ (to 2 decimal places)

- If you plot the graph of a linear equation like $y = 4x - 3$, you will get a straight line.

Remember

Don't be scared by the letters in formulae: they are simply replacing numbers.

3. Solve these equations. Use a calculator and give your answer to 2 decimal places where appropriate.

   a) $8f + 9 = 21$

   b) $5(g - 7) = 45$

   c) $8m \div 7 = 5$

   d) $9 = 4x + 7$

4. Use inverse operations to solve $8g + 15 = 36 - 6g$

5. Solve the equation $3(y + 3) - 3(15 - y) = 0$

6. Write all the possible values for h in the following statement, if h is a whole number:

   $11 < 3h < 26$

7. Write all the possible values for v in the following statement, if v is a whole number:

   $7 < 2v + 8 < 22$

8. If the length of a field is given as L and the width is 12 metres less than the length:

   a) Write a formula for finding the width of the playing field in terms of L.

   b) Write a formula for finding the perimeter of the field.

   c) If $L = 84$ metres, what is the perimeter of the field?

Generating terms of a sequence

Vocabulary   formulae; term-to-term; position-to-term; sequence

LEVEL 5

Getting started

Generate and describe linear number sequences

- A number pattern which increases or decreases by the same amount each time is called a **linear sequence**. The amount that it increases or decreases by is known as the **common difference**.

- For example, the sequence   1·5, 1·8, 2·1, 2·4…
  is linear because the numbers increase by 0·3 each time. In other words, 0·3 is the common difference.

1. Find the common difference for each linear sequence.

   a) 90, 85, 80, 75…

   b) $\dfrac{5}{10}, \dfrac{7}{10}, \dfrac{9}{10}, \dfrac{11}{10}$…

   c) 0·4, 0·9, 1·4, 1·9…

   d) 306, 291, 276, 261…

2. Write the next three terms in each linear sequence.

   a) 15, 31, 47, 63, ___, ___, ___

   b) 9·7, 9·3, 8·9, 8·5, ___, ___, ___

   c) $\dfrac{5}{18}, \dfrac{9}{18}, \dfrac{13}{18}, \dfrac{17}{18}$, ___, ___, ___

LEVEL 6

Next steps

Generate terms of a sequence using term-to-term and position-to-term definitions

- The numbers in a number sequence are called **terms**.

- The **term-to-term rule** is the rule that tells you how to get from one term to the next term in the sequence.

- For example, in the sequence   5, 8, 11, 14…,   the term-to-term rule is +3.

- The **position-to-term rule** is the rule that takes you from the position of a term in a sequence (e.g. position 8 or the 8th term) to the actual value of that term in the sequence. It is often called the **nth term** of a sequence.

- For example, if the formula or position-to-term rule for a sequence is $3n - 2$, the first three terms of the sequence would be: 1, 4 and 7. The 45th term of the sequence would be $(3 \times 45) - 2 = 133$.

> ○ **Remember**
>
> A **linear sequence** means that the difference between the terms is always the same.

3. Write the term-to-term rule and the next five terms in each sequence.

   a) 3, 7, 11…

   b) 105, 98, 91…

   c) −225, −220, −215…

   d) 3, 6, 12…

   e) 4, 16, 64…

   f) 300, 60, 12…

4. You are told that the nth term of a sequence is: $8n + 6$

   a) Use this information to write the first five terms of the sequence.

   b) What is the term-to-term rule for this sequence?

   c) Work out the value of the 33rd term.

5. The nth term of a sequence is $4(2n - 4)$

   a) Find the first five terms of the sequence.

   b) What is the term-to-term rule for this sequence?

   c) Work out the value of the 18th term.

6. The term-to-term rule for a sequence is **divide by 3**. The fourth term of the sequence is 45.

   Find the missing terms in this sequence.

   ___, ___, ___, 45, ___, ___ …

Getting started

LEVEL 5

Generate and describe linear number sequences

- A number pattern which increases or decreases by the same amount each time is called a **linear sequence**. The amount that it increases or decreases by is known as the **common difference**.

- A linear sequence can contain positive numbers, negative numbers, fractions, decimals or percentages. As long as the difference between each term of the sequence is the same, it is a linear sequence.

1. Find the common difference for each linear sequence.

   a) –13, –8, –3…

   b) 750, 350, –50…

   c) –434, –184, 66…

2. Write the next three terms in each linear sequence.

   a) 67, 32, –3, ___, ___, ___

   b) –412, –310, –208, ___, ___, ___

   c) $\dfrac{1}{16}$, $\dfrac{6}{16}$, $\dfrac{11}{16}$, ___, ___, ___

Next steps

LEVEL 6

Write an expression for the *n*th term of an arithmetic sequence

- An arithmetic sequence has a constant difference between each of its terms.

- You can use a formula to express the relationship between the position of a term in an arithmetic sequence and the value of that term.

- The formula for finding the *n*th term of a sequence is

$$n\text{th term} = dn + (a - d)$$

where d = difference between terms, a – first term and n = term number.

- For example, for the sequence starting   5, 7·5, 10... $d = +2.5$ and $a = 5$

The nth term is: $2.5n + (5 - 2.5) = 2.5n + 2.5$

The 36th term will be: $(2.5 \times 36) + 2.5 = 92.5$

◯ Remember

A **linear sequence** is sometimes called an **arithmetic sequence**.

---

3. The first three terms of a sequence are   2, 10, 18...

   a) Write down the nth term of the sequence.

   b) Use your rule to find the 17th term.

   c) Use your rule to find the 78th term.

4. You have been asked to generate a sequence starting with the number 57 and taking away 5 each time.

   a) Write down the nth term of the sequence.

   b) Use your rule to find the 12th term.

   c) Use your rule to find the 37th term.

5. The first four terms of a sequence are   954, 909, 864, 819...

   a) What is the term-to-term rule for the sequence?

   b) Write down the nth term of the sequence.

c) Use your rule to find the 9th term.

d) Use your rule to find the 22nd term.

e) Use your rule to find the 100th term.

6. The term-to-term rule for a sequence is **multiply by 4**. The 4th term of the sequence is 448. What is the first term of the sequence?

7. The 5th, 6th and 7th terms of a sequence are   ...52, 56·5, 61...

   a) What is the term-to-term rule of the sequence?

   b) What are the first three terms of the sequence?

   c) Write the expression for finding the nth term of the sequence.

   d) Use your rule to find the 27th term.

Linear function graphs

Vocabulary   coordinates; quadrants; linear functions

LEVEL 5

Getting started

Use and interpret coordinates in all four quadrants

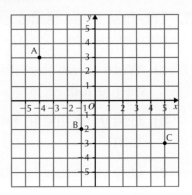

- You will be familiar with reading and plotting coordinates in grids like this one. The *x* and *y* axes of a coordinate grid can be extended into negative numbers like this:

- The coordinates are still described in the same way. For example, point A has the coordinates (–4, 3); point B has the coordinates (–1, –2) and point C has the coordinates (5, –3).

1. Write the coordinates of each point.

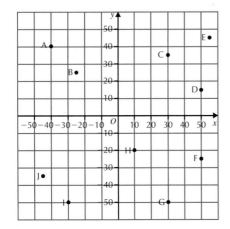

LEVEL 6

Next steps

Plot the graph of linear functions, where **y** is given explicitly in terms of **x**

- The graph of a linear function, e.g. $y = x + 3$, will be a straight line.

- To plot the graph of a linear function, complete a table of values and then plot and join the points.

- For example, for $y = x + 3$:

x	−10	1	2	3	6
y	−7	4	5	6	9

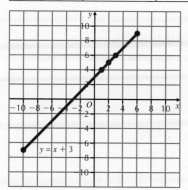

Remember

When reading coordinates, you go along the corridor (x axis) and up the stairs (y axis), meaning that the coordinates are written with the x coordinate first and then the y coordinate.

2. **a)** Copy and complete this table of values for $y = 4x - 2$

x	−8	−5	−1		4	7	
y	−34			−2			34

b) Draw the graph of $y = 4x - 2$. Don't forget to choose an appropriate scale and label your axes.

3. This graph shows a linear function.

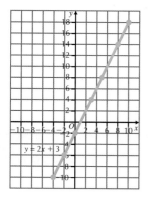

a) Copy and complete this table for the values of x and y shown on the graph.

x	−4	−2	0		5		10
y				4		14	

b) Find the equation for this linear function.

Equations for straight-line graphs

Vocabulary   coordinates; quadrants; straight-line graphs

Getting started

Use and interpret coordinates in all four quadrants

- This coordinate grid has 4 quadrants:

  Point A had the coordinates (3, 3), point B has the coordinates (−3, 4), point C has the coordinates (−2, −1) and point D has the coordinates (3, −5).

- The y coordinates of all the points on the red line are 2. The equation of the line is $y = 2$.

- The x coordinates of all the points on the blue line are −2. The equation of this line is $x = -2$.

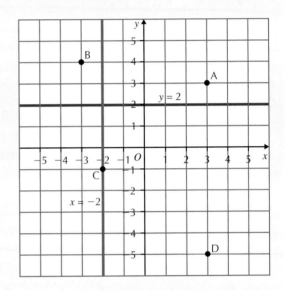

1. Write the coordinates of each point.

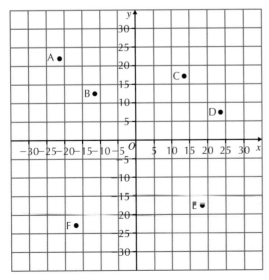

2. Find the equation of the coloured lines.

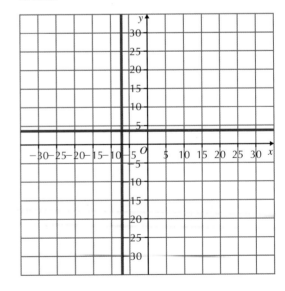

Next steps

Recognise that equations of the form $y = mx + c$ correspond to straight-line graphs

- All lines with an equation in the form $y = mx + c$ are straight lines because the value of x increases or decreases at a constant rate (m) in relation to y.

- c is a constant numerical value and is the y coordinate of where the graph will cross the x axis.

- For example, the equation $y = 2x + 3$ generates these coordinates:

  $(-1, 1)$ $(-3, -3)$ $(1, 5)$ $(2, 7)$ $(3, 9)$

  We can plot and join the coordinates to give this straight line graph which crosses the x axis at $(0, 3)$:

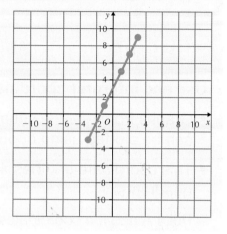

Remember

It is straightforward to find the equation of a horizontal or vertical line on a graph. Look at the axis it crosses and notice at what point it crosses it.

3. Here are the equations of some straight lines. Write down the equations whose graphs will pass through the point $(2, 5)$.

   $y = x + 3$ $y = 4x - 3$ $y = 2x + 3$ $y = 25 - x$ $y = 3x - 1$

4. Write the coordinates of the point where each equation crosses the y axis.

   $y = 3x + 2$ $y = 5x - 12$ $y = 2x + 8$ $y = 7x - 13$ $y = 4x + 8$

5. Find the equation of this straight line.

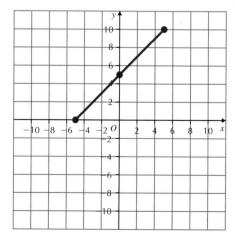

Interpreting graphs

LEVEL 5

| Vocabulary | coordinates; quadrants; graphs |

Getting started

Use and interpret coordinates in all four quadrants

- Graphs from real-life situations can be plotted using coordinates.

- This coordinate grid has 4 quadrants:

  Point A had the coordinates (3, 3), point B has the coordinates (–3, 4), point C has the coordinates (–2, –1) and point D has the coordinates (3, –5).

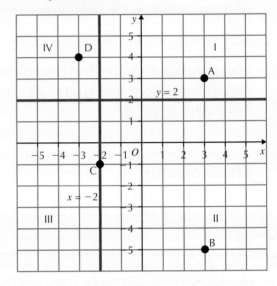

1. This graph shows the temperature of water as it is being heated.

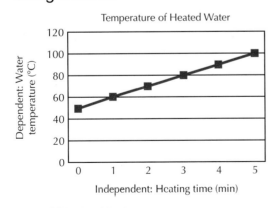

Temperature of Heated Water

a) What was the temperature of the water after 3 minutes?

b) After how long was the water at boiling point?

c) After how long was the water at 70 °C?

d) What was the temperature of the water after 3·5 minutes?

Interpret graphs arising from real-life situations

- Information from real-life observations and experiments can be plotted on a graph.

- For example, the temperature of water against time as it is heated and pulse / heart rate against time spent exercising can both be plotted on graphs.

- All good graphs will have titles and axis labels. These tell you what the graph shows, including which axis displays which information.

Remember

Check the title and the labels on the graph axes to make sure you understand what it is showing.

2. Look at this graph.

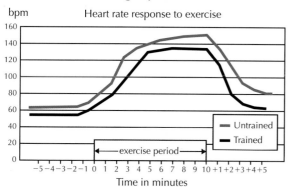

3. Look at this graph.

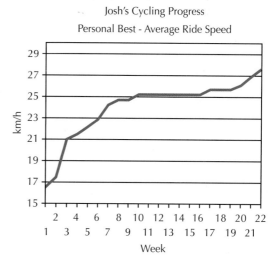

2.

a) What does the blue line of the graph show?

b) How long was the exercise period?

c) What was the bpm of the untrained athlete after 3 minutes of exercise?

d) After how many minutes of exercise was the untrained athlete's bpm at 140 bpm?

e) What can you conclude about the trained athlete's heart rate during exercise compared to the untrained athlete?

3.

a) In which week did Josh achieve his highest personal best?

b) What was Josh's personal best by week 13?

c) In week 4, what was Josh's personal best?

d) What was the increase in personal best between week 1 and week 22?

Constructing functions and plotting graphs

> **Vocabulary**   coordinates; quadrants; functions; graphs

Getting started

Use and interpret coordinates in all four quadrants

- This coordinate grid has 4 quadrants:

- Point A had the coordinates (3, 3), point B has the coordinates (–3, 4), point C has the coordinates (–2, –1) and point D has the coordinates (3, –5). B

- It is important to understand how to read coordinates in all four quadrants so that you can apply this knowledge when reading real-life graphs that cross into different quadrants.

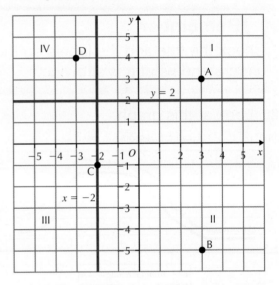

1. Look at this graph about maximum and minimum temperatures.

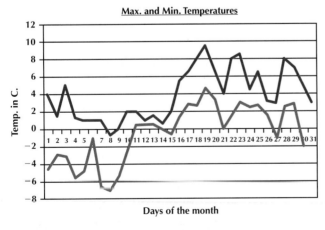

Max. and Min. Temperatures

Days of the month

a) Describe what the two lines on the graph show.

b) The data in the graph is from a town in the United Kingdom. What month of the year might it be from? Give a reason for your answer.

c) What was the highest temperature?

d) What was the lowest temperature?

e) On what days was the minimum temperature above 0 °C?

Construct functions arising from real-life problems and plot their graphs

- You will recall that in a function, there is a relationship between the input and the output. This produces pairs of values which you can plot as coordinate points and join to form a graph.

- For example, if the cost (C) of hiring a pedal boat is £30 an hour (H) plus a one-off service charge of £15, the function would read:
  $C = (£30 \times H) + £15$.

  So, to find the cost for 2 hours, the input is 2 and the output is £75.

Remember
Read the axis carefully to make sure you understand what the graph is showing.

2. The cost of hiring a village hall for a party is £50 an hour. In addition to the hourly rate, there is a charge of:

   - £25 to cover the cost of opening and closing the hall before and after the event

   - £65 an hour to hire the kitchen, plus £15 for cleaning.

   a) i) Write a formula to find the cost of hiring the hall only for 4 hours.

      ii) Use your formula to find this cost.

   b) i) Write a formula to find the cost of hiring the hall only for 7 hours.

      ii) Use your formula to find this cost.

   c) i) Write a formula to find the cost of hiring the hall and kitchen for 6 hours.

   ii) Use your formula to find this cost.

3. It costs £12.50 per hour to hire a surfboard.

   It costs £27.50 per hour for a surfing lesson, including surfboard hire.

   A £50 club membership fee must be paid before you can hire boards or take lessons.

   a) Show this information on a graph.

   b) Use your graph to find the cost of hiring a surfboard for 3 hours.

   c) Use your graph to find the cost of a 2-hour surfing lesson.

   d) You want to have a 1-hour surfing lesson and then hire a surfboard so that you can practise surfing for 2 hours. How much will this cost?

Algebra

Review

1. Use a table like this one to solve the equation $3y + y^3 = 89 \cdot 52$

y	$3y + y^3$	Comment
4	76	Too small
5	140	Much too big

2. A whole number plus its cube equals 222.

   a) Write an equation for this using algebra.

   b) What is the number?

3. Solve the equation $6r + 56 = 9r + 38$

4. Amelia is doing a sponsored swim. She has found the following formula for calculating how much sponsor money she will receive:

$$A = £7.40L$$

   where A is the total amount of sponsor money and L is the number of lengths she swims.

   a) Find A if L is 56

   b) Find L if A is £111

5. Find the term-to-term rule for each sequence.

   a) 359, 311, 263, 215…

   b) −111, −98, −85, −72…

   c) 3, 5·5, 8, 10·5…

6. A sequence has the nth term: $6(2n - 8)$

   a) What are the first three terms of the sequence?

   b) What is the 57th term of the sequence?

7. The first four terms of a sequence are: 5, 8, 11, 14...

    a) Find the *n*th term.

    b) What is the 67th term of the sequence?

8. Copy and complete this table of values for $y = 15 - 2x$

x	−8	−5	−1	3	4	7	9	11
y								

9. Here are the equations of some straight lines.

    $y = 2x$ $y = x + 3$ $y = x + 2$ $y = 4 - x$ $y = 3x + 2$ $y = 3x - 2$

    Which lines pass through the point (2, 4)?

10. Work out the equation of each of these straight lines.

a)
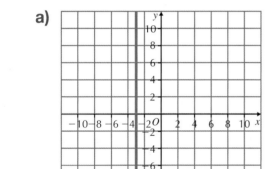

b)
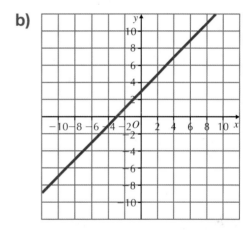

c)
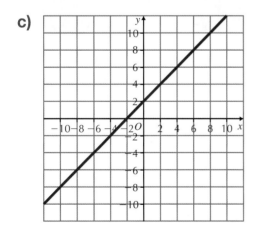

d)
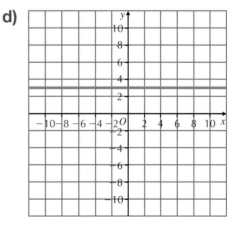

Unit 17 — Classifying quadrilaterals

| Vocabulary | lines of symmetry; angles; order of rotational symmetry; geometric properties |

LEVEL 5

Getting started

Use a range of properties of 2D and 3D shapes and identify all the symmetries of 2D shapes

- You can use mirror lines to identify **lines of symmetry** in shapes. When one side of the shape is the same as the other side along the mirror line, it is a line of symmetry.

- **Rotational symmetry** is the number of times that a shape fits back in to itself when turned all the way round.

- For example, this cross has rotational symmetry of order 4 as it fits into itself 4 times when it is rotated through a complete turn.

1.

   a) Name each of these shapes.

   b) Say whether each shape is 2D or 3D.

   c) Describe the angles and sides of each 2D shape.

2. I am a 3D shape. I have 1 curved face, 1 circular face and 1 vertex. What am I?

3. Write the order of rotational symmetry of each shape.

Next steps

Classify shapes by their geometric properties

- You need to be able to identify and use these geometric properties to classify shapes:
    - symmetries in shapes
    - numbers and lengths of sides
    - angle size.

- For example, you could classify shapes in the following ways:
    - Shapes with two sets of parallel sides, e.g.

    - Shapes with two angles the same, e.g.

    - Shapes that have sets of equal sides, e.g.

○ Remember
Use the clues you are given to visualise the shapes in your head.

4.

3D shape with 1+ vertex	3D shape with no vertex	2D shape with 2 sets of equal sides	2D shape with one set of equal sides

a) Copy the table and use it to classify these shapes:

   equilateral triangle   square-based pyramid   trapezium   rectangle

   arrowhead   sphere   cylinder   cuboid   square   irregular quadrilateral

b) Which shape does not fit into the table?

5. I am a 3D shape with 6 faces, 8 vertices and 4 sides of equal length. What could I be?

Solve problems using a range of properties

> **Vocabulary** angle sum; triangles; parallel lines; intersecting lines; polygons; angles

Getting started

Know and use the angle sum of a triangle and of angles at a point

- You can use these rules to work out missing angles.

  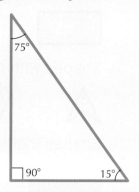

  - The angle sum of a triangle is the total value of all the angles in a triangle which is always equal to 180°. For example,
    90° + 75° + 15° = 180°

  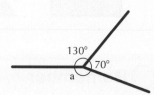

  - Angles that meet at a point add up to 360°.
    For example,
    a = 360° − (130° + 70°) = 160°

  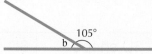

  - Angles on a straight line add up to 180°.
    For example,
    b = 180° − 105° = 75°

1. Find the value of angle m.

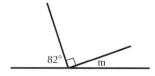

2. Find the value of r in this triangle.

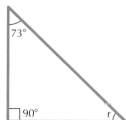

Use the properties of angles, of parallel and intersecting lines, and of triangles and other polygons

- Parallel lines stay an equal distance apart from each other and never meet.

  _____

  _____

○ **Remember**

The internal angles of a triangle add up to 180°.

3. a) What is the missing angle in this shape?

   b) How do you know?

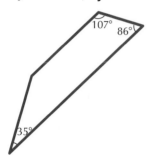

4. What are the interior angles of this octagon?

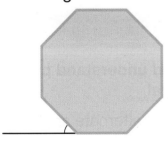

5. Write a set of clues to describe a heptagon using information about angles and lines.

6.

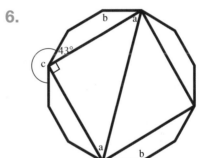

   a) What is the value of angle a?

   b) What is the value of angle b?

   c) What is the value of angle c?

Vocabulary	2D shapes; 3D shapes; symmetries; quadrilateral; triangle; proofs

LEVEL 5

Getting started

Use a range of properties of 2D and 3D shapes and identify all the symmetries of 2D shapes

- The internal angles of a quadrilateral always add up to 360°. This is the same as the number of degrees in a complete circle.

- The internal angles of a triangle add up to 180°.

1. Work out the size of m in this regular trapezium.

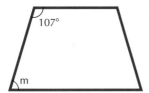

2. Work out the size of angle r in this triangle.

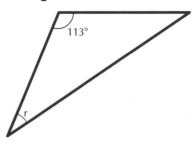

LEVEL 6

Next steps

Identify alternate and corresponding angles and understand proofs of the angle sum of a triangle and a quadrilateral

- You need to be able to identify corresponding and alternate angles along lines.

- For example,
  a and c are opposite angles
  a and m are corresponding angles
  b and p are alternate angles

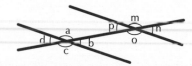

> ○ **Remember**
>
> You can apply the rules you know about angles in triangles and quadrilaterals to find the angles in triangular and quadrilateral faces of 3D shapes.

3. Which angle corresponds with angle a in this diagram?

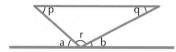

4. Work out the angles marked with letters in this diagram.

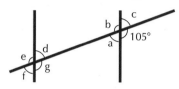

5. This diagram shows a hexagon:

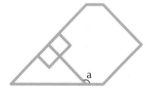

a) Is it a regular hexagon? Give a reason for your answer.

b) Use the triangle to work out angle a.

6. Here is a rhombus:

a) Find the value of angle a.

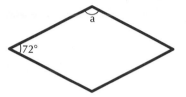

b) A diagonal is drawn to divide the rhombus in half.

Copy the diagram and mark on all of the angles in the triangles.

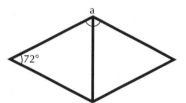

2D representations of 3D objects

Vocabulary   2D shapes; 3D shapes; symmetries; net

Getting started

Use a range of properties of 2D and 3D shapes and identify all the symmetries of 2D shapes

- 3D shapes can be opened out to create a flat net.

- For example:

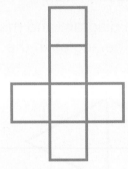

one possible net
of a cube

a net of a square-based
pyramid

1. What are these shapes?

   a) A 3D shape with 6 vertices, 9 edges and 5 faces

   b) A 2D shape with 2 edges the same length, 2 sets of identical angles and 1 set of parallel lines

   c) A 3D shape with no vertices, no edges and 1 face

   d) A 3D shape with 12 pentagonal faces, 20 vertices and 30 edges

2. Draw four different nets for a cube.

Next steps

Use 2D representations of 3D objects

- Architects use 2D drawings to help them design buildings. They draw the building from each side and from the top.

- The view from the top (like a birds-eye view) is called the **plan**.
- The view from the front and sides are called the **elevations**.
- Representations of 3D shapes can be drawn on isometric grids.

> **Remember**
> A net of a 3D shape is a flat representation that can be folded to create the final shape.

3. Here is the net of a 3D shape:

   Draw the shape on an isometric grid.

   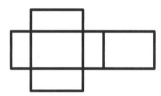

4. Here is the net of a 3D shape:

   Draw the shape on an isometric grid.

   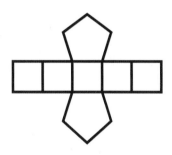

5. If four cuboids were placed together so that the plan view looked like this:

   Shape A

   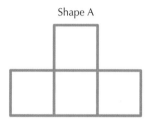

   a) How many edges would the final 3D shape have?

   b) How many vertices would the final 3D shape have?

   c) How many faces would the final 3D shape have?

Enlarging 2D shapes

Vocabulary	position; movement; transformation; enlarging; centre of enlargement; scale factor; rotation; translation; reflection

Getting started

Reason about position and movement and transform shapes

- There are three main types of transformation:

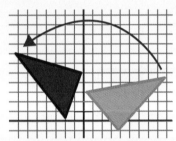 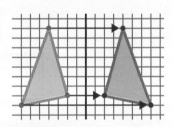 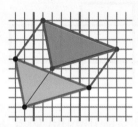

- **Rotation** a shape is turned around a point
- **Reflection** a shape is reflected in a mirror line
- **Translation** a shape is moved horizontally and/or vertically

1. Describe by how many squares each shape been translated.

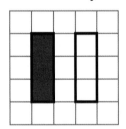 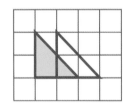 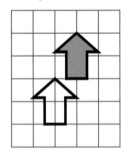

2. Copy each shape and rotate it 90° anticlockwise around point A.

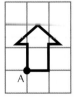 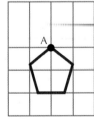 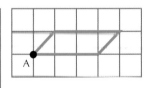

Enlarge 2D shapes given a centre of enlargement and a positive whole number scale factor

- The scale factor tells us by how much the object has been enlarged.

- For example,

P'Q' = 3 × PQ

Q'R' = 3 × QR

R'S' = 3 × RS

S'P' = 3 × SP

◯ Remember

Learn the three main types of transformation so that you do not get confused!

3. Copy this shape onto squared paper. Enlarge it by a scale factor of 5 using X as the centre of enlargement.

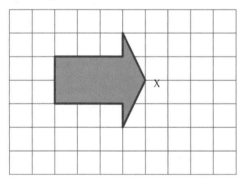

4. This regular pentagon has a perimeter of 52·5 cm.

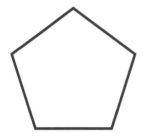

It is enlarged by a scale factor of 1·5

a) What is the length of each side in the original shape?

b) What is the length of each side in the enlarged shape?

c) What is the perimeter of the enlarged shape?

5. A shape is enlarged by a scale factor of 8.

a) One angle of the original shape is 154°. What is the size of this angle on the enlarged shape?

b) One side of the original shape is 4·5 cm. What is the length of this side on the enlarged shape?

c) A different side of the enlarged shape is 96 cm. What was the length of the side on the original shape?

Making congruent images of shapes

> **Vocabulary**   position; movement; transformation; rotation; translation; reflection; congruent image

Getting started

Reason about position and movement and transform shapes

- There are three main types of transformation.

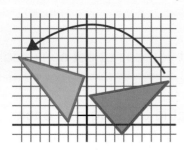

Rotation

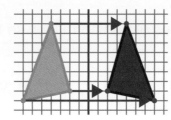

Reflection

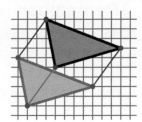

Translation

1. Draw a rectangle with an area of 6 squares on squared paper.

   a) Rotate the rectangle 90° clockwise and draw the image.

   b) Draw a mirror line and reflect the original rectangle in it.

   c) Translate the image from part (b) 2 squares down and 5 squares to the right.

2. Draw an irregular quadrilateral with an area of 11 squares on squared paper.

   a) Rotate the quadrilateral 180° and draw the image.

   b) Draw a horizontal mirror line. Reflect the rotated image in this mirror line.

   c) Translate the original image 3 squares up and 4 squares to the left.

Know that translations, rotations and reflections preserve length and angle and map objects onto congruent images

- When two shapes are **congruent**, all their corresponding sides and angles are equal.

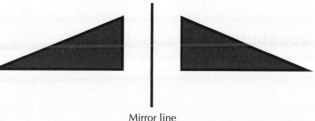

Mirror line

- When a shape is reflected in a mirror, translated or rotated the image is the same size and shape as the original object, i.e. they are congruent.

- Enlarged shapes are not congruent.

◯ Remember

When a shape is rotated, reflected or translated, the original shape and the image are the same shape and size.

3. The arrow ABCDE is reflected in a mirror line. This gives the shaded arrow which is congruent to arrow ABCDE.

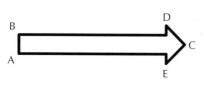

Congruent image

a) Make a copy of ABCDE and its reflected image. Draw a dashed line to show the mirror line.

b) Copy the letters onto arrow ABCDE and mark the corresponding letters on the congruent image using a dash.

4. a) Which of the following shapes are congruent to A?

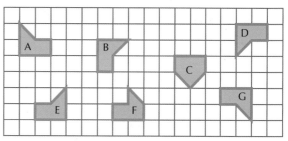

b) Describe the transformation that has created each congruent shape, e.g. a translation of 2 squares right and 1 square down.

LEVEL 5

Getting started

Measure and draw angles to the nearest degree

- You need to be able to use a protractor to draw and measure angles accurately.

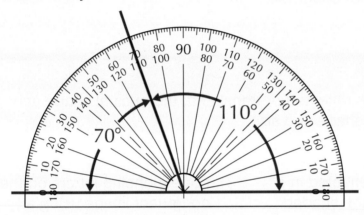

1. Use a protractor to draw and label the following angles:

   a) 45°

   b) 90°

   c) 78°

   d) 113°

   e) 162°

   f) An acute angle of your choice

   g) An obtuse angle of your choice

   h) A reflex angle of your choice

LEVEL 6

Next steps

Use straight edge and compasses to do standard constructions

- If you are asked to **construct** a shape or angle, you must draw it accurately using a pencil, ruler and compass. You cannot measure angles with a protractor to construct them.

- Perpendicular lines are lines which are at right angles to each another:

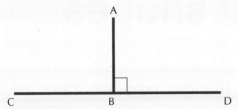

AB is perpendicular to line CD

- You need to know how to bisect lines and angles:

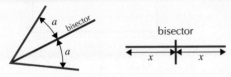

○ Remember

Line your protractor up carefully with the arms of the angle you are measuring.

2. Draw a pentagon with sides 7 cm and angles 108°.

3. Draw a triangle with one right angle, one angle of 57° and one side of 5 cm.

4. Use a ruler and compass to construct a trapezium. Mark the two perpendicular lines.

5. a) Draw a scalene triangle.

   b) Use a ruler and compasses to construct the bisector of each angle of your triangle.

c) What do you notice about where the lines cross one another?

6. Use a ruler, protractor and compasses to draw this shape accurately.

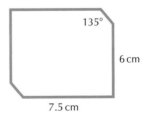

Unit 24 Deduce and use formulae for area of 2D shapes

Vocabulary rectangle; formulae; triangle; parallelogram; area

⑤ Getting started

Use the formula for the area of a rectangle

- The area of a rectangle can be found by multiplying the width by the length.

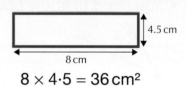

$$8 \times 4{\cdot}5 = 36 \text{ cm}^2$$

1. Draw four rectangles with different widths and lengths but the same area.

2. Work out the area of this shape:

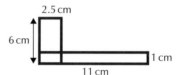

⑥ Next steps

Deduce and use the formulae for the area of a triangle and a parallelogram

- Area of a triangle

  Area $= \dfrac{1}{2} \times$ base $\times$ perpendicular height

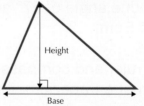

- Area of a parallelogram

  Area $=$ base $\times$ height

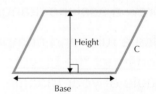

○ Remember
Check for overlaps when finding the area of shapes made up of squares or rectangles.

3. Find the area of this parallelogram:

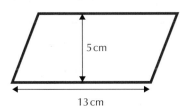

5 cm

13 cm

4. Find the area of this triangle:

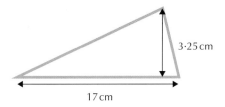

3·25 cm

17 cm

5. Look at this diagram.

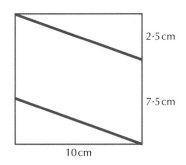

2·5 cm

7·5 cm

10 cm

a) Work out the area of each triangle.

b) Work out the area of the parallelogram.

c) Work out the area of the square. What do you notice?

6. A triangle has an area of 52·25 cm² and a base of 19 cm. What is the perpendicular height of the triangle?

7. A parallelogram has an area of 63 cm² and a perpendicular height of 18 cm. What is the length of the base of the parallelogram?

8. Work out the area of:

a) triangle A

b) triangle B

c) triangle C.

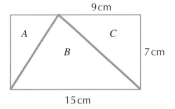

9 cm

A

B

C

7 cm

15 cm

Vocabulary volume; surface area; cuboid; perimeter; area

⑤ Getting started

Distinguish area from perimeter

- Finding the perimeter of a shape means finding the distance all around the outside of it. So if each side of this pentagon is 6 cm, the perimeter is $6 + 6 + 6 + 6 + 6 = 30$ cm.

- For example, the perimeter of this trapezium is $8 + 12 + 5 + 5 = 30$ cm.

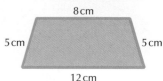

1.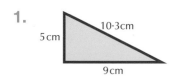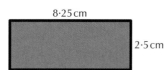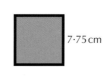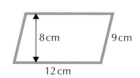

   a) Name each shape.

   b) Find the perimeter of each shape.

   c) Find the area of each shape.

⑥ Next steps

Calculate volumes and surface areas of cuboids

- To find the volume of a cuboid, work out the area of one of the rectangular faces and multiply it by the depth of the cuboid.

- For example, to find the area of this cuboid:

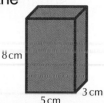

   Work out the area of the shaded rectangular face:
   $8 \times 5 = 40$ cm²

Multiply this by the depth of the cuboid to get the volume: 40 × 3 = 120 cm³

- The surface area of a shape is the total area of all the outside of the shape.

- To find the surface area of a cuboid, find the area of each rectangular face and add them together. The faces are in pairs so you can multiply by 2.

◯ Remember

Perimeter means the distance all around the outside of a shape. Area is the total space inside the shape.

2. Calculate the volume of this cuboid:

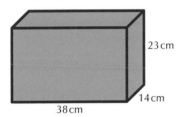
23 cm
14 cm
38 cm

3. Sketch the cuboid from question 2 and mark on the lengths of all edges. Use your diagram to work out the surface area of the cuboid.

4. What is the volume of a cube with sides of 13·6 cm?

13·6 cm

5. These two cuboids have the same volume.

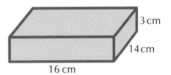
3 cm
14 cm
16 cm

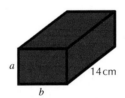
a
14 cm
b

Write down possible measurements for a and b.

6. You are shown two different boxes. They are both cuboids and they both have a volume of 432 cm³ and a depth of 9 cm. Write down possible measurements for each side of each box if all measurements are whole numbers.

Circumference and area of circles

> **Vocabulary**   circumference; formulae; radius; area; circle; pi (π); perimeter; area

Getting started

LEVEL 5

Distinguish area from perimeter

- The perimeter of a shape is the distance all the way around the outside.

- The area of a shape is the amount of space inside the shape. To find the area of a square or rectangle, multiply the width by the length.

- For example, the perimeter of this shape is
11 cm + 11 cm + 3 cm + 3 cm = 28 cm. The area
is 11 cm × 3 cm = 33 cm.

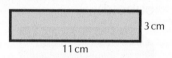

- To find the area of a compound shape, divide it into rectangles and squares.

1. Look at this shape:

    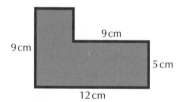

    a) Work out the missing measurements.

    b) Work out the perimeter of the shape.

    c) Work out the area of the shape.

Next steps

LEVEL 6

Know and use the formulae for the circumference and area of a circle

- You need to know these parts of a circle:

- To find the area and circumference of a circle, use these formulae:

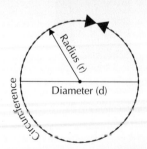

area = $\pi \times r^2$

circumference = $2 \times \pi \times r$

- Pi (π) is a mathematical constant and is approximately equal to 3·14159.

🔍 Remember

Perimeter means the distance all around the outside of a shape. Area is the total space inside the shape.

2. The pizza has a diameter of 26 cm.

 a) What is the circumference of the pizza?

 b) What is the area of the pizza?

3. These two circles share the same centre. The larger circle has a radius of 8 cm and the smaller circle has a radius of 1·5 cm.

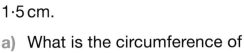

 a) What is the circumference of each circle?

 b) What is the area of each circle?

 c) What is the area of the orange area?

4. The diagram shows a quarter of a circle.

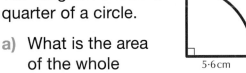

5·6 cm

 a) What is the area of the whole circle?

 b) What is the perimeter of the whole circle?

 c) What is the area of the segment shown?

 d) What is the perimeter of the segment shown?

5. The circumference of this bike wheel is 128 cm.

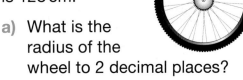

 a) What is the radius of the wheel to 2 decimal places?

 b) What is the diameter of the wheel to 2 decimal places?

 c) What is the area of the bike wheel?

Review

1. Here is a triangle.

   a) Measure each line and then draw a triangle the same size. Write all the lengths you measured on your triangle.

   b) Mark on the perpendicular height and measure with a ruler.

   c) Find the perimeter of the triangle.

   d) Calculate the area of the triangle.

2. Work out the angles A, B, C and D.

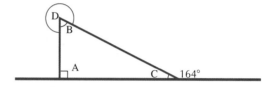

3. Work out the size of the lettered angles.

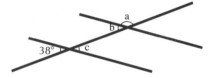

4. a) What is the angle of n?

   b) What is the angle of q?

   c) What is the angle of m?

   d) What is the angle of p?

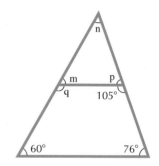

5. Draw a net of a square-based pyramid.

6. On isometric paper, draw the 3D shape that would be made from this net.

7. Point B on this shape is at (2, −1)

   a) Copy the grid and translate the T-shape so that point B is at (−1, 4).

   b) How many squares has it been translated in each direction?

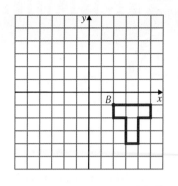

8. Write down the coordinates of the congruent image if this shape was reflected in:

   a) the x axis?

   b) the y axis?

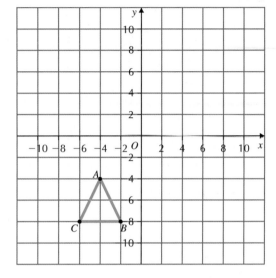

9. Draw a triangle with angles 62°, 73° and 45°.

10. A tractor tyre has a diameter of 195 cm.

    a) Calculate the circumference of the tyre.

    b) Calculate the area of the tyre.

11. A box is wrapped ready for a birthday.

    One of its faces is rectangular and measures 24 cm × 15 cm. The box is 8 cm deep.

    a) Sketch the box and label all of its edges.

    b) Calculate the volume of the box.

    c) Work out the total surface area of the wrapped box.

Handling data

Design a survey or experiment

Vocabulary	data; survey; experiment; table; results

LEVEL 5

Getting started

Plan how to collect data to answer questions

- **Data** is another word for information.

- We usually collect data for a particular purpose.

- Think about how you will collect your data, e.g. in a table or tally chart, and make sure that the answers to the questions that you ask will give you the information that you need.

1. Ryan wants to find out how much ice cream is sold by one ice cream van when it is parked in the same place on different days during the month. Draw a table that he could use to collect his data.

2. Mandy wants to know how many cars park in the school car park (on average) at different times of the day during term-time.

   a) How could she carry out this survey?

   b) What would she need to consider?

   c) How could she collect her results?

LEVEL 6

Next steps

Design a survey or experiment

- A survey is one way of collecting information (data). It could be a paper or online questionnaire that individuals are asked to complete or a series of questions asked by an interviewer who records responses.

> 🔍 **Remember**
> Think through each aspect of your survey or experiment and plan how you will collect your results.

3. Max wants to find out the favourite crisp flavour (from a selection of five main flavours) of the boys in his school.

   a) Draw the table he could use to collect his data.

   b) How could he extend his study to take other sample groups into consideration?

4. A TV channel wants to carry out a survey to help decide which programme to put on at 4:00 pm every weekday afternoon.

   a) What questions should they ask on their survey?

   b) Who should they include in their sample group (e.g. ages)?

5. All children should be at school by 9:00 am. Jane wants to find out why parents are sometimes late bringing their children to school. She decides to carry out a survey at the school gate between 8:40 am and 8:55 am and ask parents two questions:

   • Are you ever late bringing your child to school?

   • If so, why?

   How could you improve Jane's survey so she gets a better understanding of why parents are sometimes late bringing their children to school?

6. A group of children carried out a survey to answer the question:

   'What is your favourite game to play at playtime?'

   They decided to ask this question to children who were sitting on the benches or chatting with their friends round the edge of the playground. They did this at every playtime over a two-week period. The table shows their results.

Favourite game	Chatting with friends	Tag	Football	Ball games	Sitting quietly on my own
Number who gave this as an answer	87	0	2	1	34

   a) What is wrong with the way that they carried out their research?

   b) Suggest how they could improve their survey.

   c) Explain the results in the table, based on the survey that was carried out.

Collecting data

| **Vocabulary** | data; data collection; tables; raw data; primary data |

LEVEL 5

Getting started

Plan how to collect data to answer questions

- Data is usually collected to help answer a particular question.

- When data has been collected, it can be analysed and used to help make decisions about important issues.

- For example, in question 1, Tim could pass the information he collects to the class teacher, who could use it to find ways to overcome obstacles to reading at home.

1. Tim wants to find out why some children in his class of 26 children read at home and why others do not. He decides to ask 5 children at random the following question:

   "Do you read at home?"

   a) What is wrong with Tim's survey?

   b) How would you carry out a survey to answer this question?

2. Chan is researching favourite sports of the children in his class. He draws the table to the right and plans to collect his data using a tally method.

What is your favourite sport?		
	Football	Rugby	Other
Number of children who answered each option:			

a) Suggest how Chan could improve his table so that he gets a better set of data to answer the question.

b) Draw a table that Chan could use to collect data to answer this question.

Next steps

Construct tables for sets of raw data

- Raw data is the data that has been collected, for example from a survey, before it has been ordered or analysed.

- When you design a survey or experiment, you need to think about how you will collect the raw data so that it will be quick and clear.

- You need to be able to use this data in the next stage of data handling: analysis.

Remember
Think about the type of data you will collect and how you will record it.

3. Siobhan wants to find out the colours of each vehicle that drives past her house over a one-hour period.

   a) What does she need to decide about colours before she carries out the survey?

   b) Draw a table that she could use to collect her data.

4. Mr Errington's class are monitoring the sound levels in the classroom during a day. They decide to take a reading every half an hour from 9:00 am. Draw a table that they could use to collect their data.

5. The headteacher of a school wants to compare the test scores of 15 children. Each child sat Test A and Test B and each test was out of 40 marks. Draw a table that she could use to record the data.

6. You have been asked to record data to answer the question:

   "How often does each child in the school do extra-curricular sport during the week?"

   a) Describe your sample group.

   b) What questions will you ask on your survey? (Think about the groups you will use in your analysis.)

   c) Write a method to show how you will carry out your survey.

   d) Draw the table you will use to collect your data for each question.

Pie charts

Vocabulary   pie charts; categorical data; graphs; diagrams; percentage

LEVEL 5

Getting started

Interpret graphs and diagrams, including pie charts, and draw conclusions

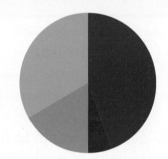

- Pie charts represent data using sectors of a circle.

- The whole circle (or pie) is worth 100% or 1 whole.

- We can use this to estimate the fraction or percentage of each sector or slice of the pie.

1. The following pie chart shows 200 responses to the question:

"Do you like coming to school?"

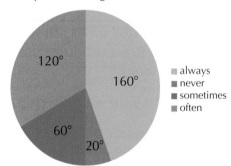

- always
- never
- sometimes
- often

a) What was the most popular response?

b) About what fraction of the children said they "often" like coming to school?

c) About what percentage said they "never" like coming to school?

d) Write down one other conclusion you could draw from this pie chart.

LEVEL 6

Next steps

Select and construct pie charts for categorical data

- Categorical data can be sorted according to distinct categories. The categories cannot overlap and the values must belong in only one of the categories.

- For example:

  o coloured counters can be sorted into categories based on colours – red, blue, green, yellow…

- To construct a pie chart:

  1. Find the total number of items represented on the pie chart.

  2. Find the fraction that each category is of the total number of items.

  3. Multiply each fraction by 360° to work out the angle of each segment.

◯ Remember

Sometimes you are told the number of people or things that the pie chart represents. The total of the pie chart is always 100% or one whole.

2. The table shows data that has been collected from a class to find children's favourite crisp flavour from a given number of choices.

	Salt and vinegar	Ready salted	Cheese and onion	Sour cream and chive	Chilli	Salt and black pepper	Chicken
Boys	8	9	13	12	5	9	2
Girls	5	13	8	10	8	13	0

a) What three **different** pie charts could you draw from this data?

b) Write two conclusions that you could draw from each of the three sets of data.

3. The following data has been collected in response to the question:

"How did you travel to school this morning?"

The results are given as percentages.

	Bus	Car	Van	Taxi	Cycle	Walk
Percentage who chose each option	20%	33%	2%	6%	18%	21%

a) Draw a pie chart to show this data. (Remember to convert the percentages to degrees. 100% = 360°)

b) Use your pie chart to find the fraction of children who travelled by car.

c) Which was the most popular form of transport?

d) About what fraction travelled to school by bus or car?

e) About what fraction travelled to school by non-motorised transport?

Bar charts and frequency diagrams

> **Vocabulary** bar charts; frequency diagrams; discrete data; continuous data; quantitative data; qualitative data

Getting started

Interpret graphs and diagrams, including pie charts, and draw conclusions

- Data can be represented using different graphs and diagrams.

- Bar charts are often used to compare two or more values.

- Pie charts are used to compare parts of a whole.

- Line graphs are used to track changes over time.

- Scatter diagrams can be used to determine the relationship between two variables.

1. This bar chart shows the answers given to the question:

   "Which of these five authors is your favourite?"

   80 adults, 80 boys and 80 girls were surveyed.

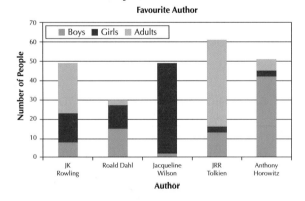

   a) Who is the most popular author over all?

   b) Which author is the most popular amongst the girls?

   c) Which author is the most popular amongst the boys?

   d) Which author is the most popular amongst the adults?

   e) Which author is the most popular amongst the children?

   f) Which author is the least popular author amongst the children?

   g) Which author is the least popular author amongst the adults?

   h) About how many girls chose JRR Tolkien as their favourite author?

Select and construct bar charts and frequency diagrams for discrete and continuous data

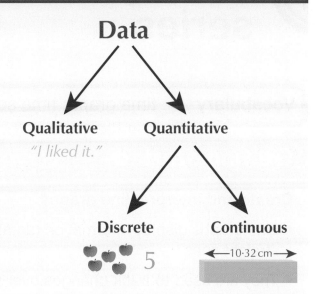

Data

Qualitative
"I liked it."

Quantitative

Discrete

Continuous
←—10·32 cm—→

5

- Discrete data can only take certain values, e.g. shoe size can only be whole or half numbers: you cannot have, e.g. 4·6.

- Continuous data can take any value within a range, e.g. height: 158·1 cm, 158·15 cm, 158·2 cm.

- Frequency diagrams, such as bar charts, show how often something happens.

◯ Remember

Think about what the data is showing and draw conclusions based on the question and sample group.

2. State whether the data collected from surveys on each of these topics would be discrete or continuous.

   a) Shoe size   **c)** Height   **e)** Room temperature

   b) Weight   **d)** Favourite pets (tally chart for given options)

3. You are shown this data table:

Shoe sizes	12–2	2–4	4–7	7–15
Number of adults with that shoe size	104	87	67	46

   a) What type of data is shown?

   b) What is wrong with the data?

   c) Suggest some groups that you could use to collect more meaningful data.

   d) What type of chart or graph could you use to display the corrected data?

Time graphs for time series

> **Vocabulary**   time graph; time series; line graph

Getting started

Level 5

Create and interpret line graphs

- Line graphs display information (data) as a series of points joined by straight lines.

- They are used to track changes over periods of time (hours, days, weeks, months or years).

1. This line graph shows the number of children in a school over a number of years.

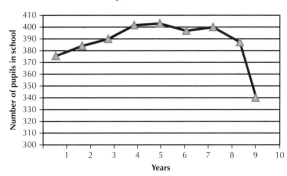

a) Is the data continuous or discrete?

b) How many children were in the school in year 6?

c) What was the decrease in numbers between years 7 and 9?

d) How many children were in the school at the start of the data collection?

Next steps

Level 6

Select and construct simple time graphs for time series

- Time series data is collected over a period of time. This period of time could be a series of seconds, minutes, hours, days, weeks, months, years or decades.

- Graphs of time series are drawn as line graphs, for example:

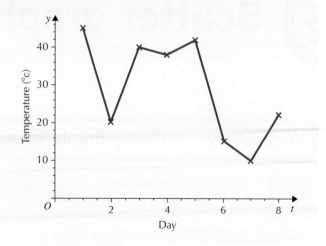

> ## Remember
> Check the axes of the graphs to see what the data is showing.

2. Ask an adult to boil a kettle and pour water from it into a cup. Put a thermometer into the cup. Record the temperature of the water in the cup every 2 minutes for a 20-minute period. Keep the thermometer in the same place throughout.

   a) Draw the table you will use to collect your data.

   b) Record your data as you work.

   c) Draw a time graph for your data.

3. This data shows the amount of rainfall during one week.

Day	1	2	3	4	5	6	7
Amount of rainfall (mm)	4	25	32	28·5	12	5	0·5

   a) Is the data discrete or continuous?

   b) Draw a time graph to show this data. Remember to label your axes carefully.

4. Write down three different ways that you could collect time series data for temperature.

Scatter graphs

Vocabulary	scatter graph; line graph; construct

Getting started

LEVEL 5

Create and interpret line graphs

- A line chart or line graph displays information (data) as a series of points joined by straight lines.

1. Draw a line graph for this data.

Age of child (in years)	5	6	7	8	9	10
Average height (in cm)	98	103	110	117	121	127

Next steps

LEVEL 6

Select and construct scatter graphs

- You can use a scatter graph to identify connections or correlations between two sets of data.

- A line of best fit can be drawn on a scatter graph. This will show you whether a piece of data value is above or below average.

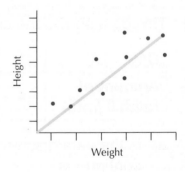

- You need to be able to recognise and describe these types of correlation:

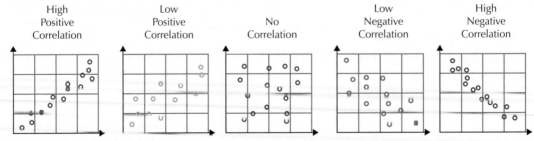

| High Positive Correlation | Low Positive Correlation | No Correlation | Low Negative Correlation | High Negative Correlation |

2. This graph shows two sets of test scores for 6-year-olds in English during 2013.

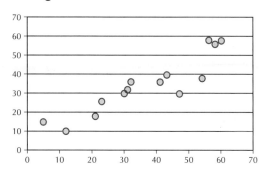

a) Suggest a suitable title for this graph.

b) Suggest suitable labels for the graph axes.

c) Describe the correlation shown in this graph.

d) What did the child who scored 5 on one test, score on the other test?

e) What did the child who scored 60 on one test, score on the other test?

3. The table below shows the height and weight of nine 10-year-olds.

Height (in cm)	120	131	125	120	120	121	123	128	118
Weight (in kg)	28	35	30	31	28.5	30	30·5	32	28

a) Draw a scatter graph to show this data

b) What can you say about the correlation?

c) Draw a line of best fit on your graph.

4. The table shows the age and weekly grocery spend of 9 shoppers.

Age (years)	28	29	30	31	32	33	34	35	36
Average weekly spending on groceries (£)	95	180	205	50	101	285	62·50	99	240

a) Draw a scatter graph to show this data. Remember to label your axes carefully and include a title.

b) Draw a line of best fit.

c) Identify the correlation shown by this data.

Finding mutually exclusive outcomes

Vocabulary	probability; mutually exclusive outcomes; possibilities; outcomes; experimental evidence; systematic

Getting started

Find possibilities based on equally likely outcomes or experimental evidence

- Outcomes of an event are equally likely when they all have the same chance of occurring.

- For example, throwing a coin has two possible outcomes: heads or tails. Each outcome has an equal chance of occurring (assuming the coins have not been tampered with) and so the probability of each outcome is $\frac{1}{2}$.

1. Write down three events with three equally likely outcomes.

2. If a 10-sided dice was rolled once, write down the probability of rolling a:

   a) 6

   b) 10

   c) 4

   Explain these probabilities.

Next steps

Find and record all possible mutually exclusive outcomes for single events and two successive events in a systematic way

- Mutually exclusive events are those that can not occur at the same time as each other.

- For example, tossing a coin and getting a head and tail on the same toss or turning over a playing card and having a Queen and a King.

- A sample space diagram is a useful way to record the outcome of more than one event.

- For example, this sample space diagram shows the outcomes of rolling a dice and tossing a coin:

	1	2	3	4	5	6
Head (H)	H, 1	H, 2	H, 3	H, 4	H, 5	H, 6
Tail (T)	T, 1	T, 2	T, 3	T, 4	T, 5	T, 6

- You can then use this to work out the probability of each outcome.

○ Remember
Think carefully about the possible number of outcomes for each event.

3. Use the sample space diagram above to answer these questions.

   a) Write down the probability of obtaining a 3 on the dice and a head on the coin.

   b) Write down the probability of obtaining a 4 on the dice and a tail on the coin.

   c) Write down the probability of rolling an even number on the dice and a tail on the coin.

4. One bag contains three counters: 1 red, 1 blue and 1 yellow. A second bag contains three number cards: 1 each of 5, 7 and 9. One item is taken at random from each bag.

   a) List all the possible outcomes.

   b) Find the probability that the counter is blue and the digit card is number 7.

   c) Find the probability that the counter is yellow and the digit card is **not** 9.

   d) Find the probability that the counter is not blue and the card is not number 5.

5. Six cards with letters on (P, Q, R, S, T and U) are placed on the table face down. Two of the cards are picked up at random.

   a) Write down all the possible outcomes.

   b) What is the probability that P and S are turned over?

   c) What is the probability that T and T are turned over?

   d) What is the probability that R is one of the cards?

The sum of mutually exclusive outcomes

> **Vocabulary**   probability; mutually exclusive outcomes; probability scale

Getting started

Understand and use the probability scale from 0 to 1; Find probabilities based on equally likely outcomes or experimental evidence

- The chances of any event occurring can be shown on a probability scale from 0 to 1.

- Events that will never occur, i.e. events that are **impossible**, have a probability of 0.

- Events that are **certain** to occur have a probability of 1.

- Events that have an even chance of happening have a probability of $\frac{1}{2}$.

1. Mark each of these events on a probability scale (using decimals or fractions).

   a) It will not rain in England for five years.

   b) I will finish my homework tonight.

   c) I will meet a person who has climbed Mount Everest.

   d) I will get run over by a giraffe driving a car.

   e) It will snow at the North Pole at least one day this year.

   f) It will snow and be 25 °C at the same time on the same day.

Next steps

Know and use the fact that the sum of probabilities of all mutually exclusive outcomes is 1

- Mutually exclusive outcomes can not occur at the same time as each other, for example raining and not raining or getting a 1 and getting a 3 when throwing a dice.

- When the outcomes are also exhaustive, that is there are no other options, the sum of their probabilities is 1.

- For example, when throwing a dice:

$$P(1) + P(2) + P(3) + P(4) + P(5) + P(6) = 1$$

$$\frac{1}{6} + \frac{1}{6} + \frac{1}{6} + \frac{1}{6} + \frac{1}{6} + \frac{1}{6} = 1$$

> ## ◯ Remember
> Certain = 1 and impossible = 0.

2. Shruti did a traffic survey on a busy road. Her results showed that 75% of traffic was cars, 10% was lorries, 5% was motorbikes and the rest was buses. Find the probability that:

   a) the next vehicle to pass will be a lorry

   b) the next vehicle to pass will be a motorbike

   c) the next vehicle to pass will not be a bus or a lorry

   d) the next vehicle to pass will be a car or a motorbike.

3. The probability that the temperature is below 0 °C is 0·2. The probability that the temperature is below 8 °C but above 0 °C is 0·6.

   Find the probability that the temperature is:

   a) 8 °C or above

   b) below 8 °C.

4. The probability of the number of days of snow in the United Kingdom each year is shown in this table:

Number of days of snow	1	2	3	More than 3
Probability	70%	13%	5%	2%

Find the probability that:

a) there are no days of snow in a year.

b) there are at least two days of snow in a year.

Communicating results of a survey

Vocabulary   graphs; diagrams; interpretation; results

LEVEL 5

Getting started

Interpret graphs and diagrams, including pie charts, and draw conclusions

- Once a need for data has been identified, a question formed and data has been collected by survey or experiment, it is represented using graphs. These graphs can then be interpreted and conclusions drawn in response to the original question.

1. Write down three Science experiments that you could do to obtain quantitative data for analysis.

2. Here is a pie chart showing children's favourite meals. 550 children were interviewed for the survey.

   a) What is the most popular dish?

   Favourite meals

   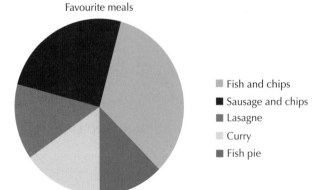

   - Fish and chips
   - Sausage and chips
   - Lasagne
   - Curry
   - Fish pie

b) What is the least popular dish?

c) About what percentage of children chose sausage and chips as their favourite dish?

d) About how many children chose dishes containing fish (fish and chips and fish pie) as their favourite dish?

e) About how many children chose lasagne as their favourite dish?

f) What percentage of children chose fish pie as their favourite dish?

Remember

Check the number of items that the pie chart represents (if you are given this information). This always represents 100%.

Communicate interpretations and results of a survey using selected tables, graphs and diagrams in support

- You need to be able to read and represent data using:
  - Tables showing tallies, numbers or grouped frequencies
  - Appropriate graphs and diagrams, including pie charts, bar charts, line graphs and scatter graphs

3. The table shows the results of a survey about how long people have lived in their current homes. 600 people from the same town were surveyed.

Number of years	0–3	4–7	8–11	12–15	16–19	20–23	24–27	28+
Number of people	205	180	150	30	15	12	5	3

a) What can you say about the general trend for housing in the town?

b) Draw a graph to show this data more clearly.

c) Use your graph to write down three conclusions that you can draw from the data.

4. A dice is rolled 300 times. The results are shown in the table below:

Outcome	Frequency
1	46
2	47
3	58
4	51
5	49
6	49

a) Draw a suitable graph to display this data.

b) Explain why you chose this graph.

c) Explain the results of this experiment, giving reasons for the frequencies.

Handling data

Review

1. Katia thinks that the popularity of different school subjects changes with age. She is going to carry out a survey to find out if this is true. Her first question is: How old are you?

    a) What other questions could she ask?

    b) Draw a table that she could use to collect her data to answer the question.

2. Four playing cards (King of Hearts, 10 of Clubs, 6 of Diamonds, Queen of Clubs) are placed face down on the table. One is picked up at random.

    Write down the probability that:

    a) it is a King and a Queen

    b) it is a Club

    c) it is a red card

    d) it is the 6 of Diamonds.

3. There are 3 different types of fruit in a bag: 8 bananas, 4 apples and 6 oranges. If 2 pieces of fruit are picked out at random, what is the probability that:

    a) neither is a banana?

    b) one is a banana and one is an orange?

    c) neither piece of fruit is an apple?

4. Kath wants to find out whether there is a correlation between the amount of sleep children have and their performance in a test. She surveys the 30 children in her class and records the results on this scatter diagram:

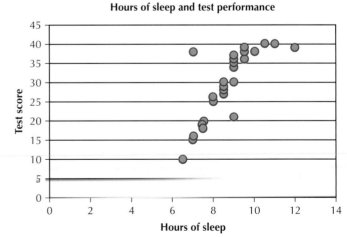

Hours of sleep and test performance

a) Describe the correlation in the graph and say what this means about the relationship between hours of sleep and marks in a test.

b) What further research might you need to do to find out if this trend is widespread?

c) What is unusual about the results of one of the children who had 7 hours sleep?

d) One child who had 9 hours sleep does not fit the trend as well as the others. Explain how this is shown in the graph.

5. These tables show the average weekly hours of exercise for men and women in one country from 2007 to 2013.

WOMEN

	2007	2008	2009	2010	2011	2012	2013
At the gym	11	11·5	11	12	13	16	14
Jogging/running	5	6	5·5	5·5	5	6·5	7
Team sports	3	3·5	3·5	4	3·5	4·5	4·5
TOTAL	19	21	20	21·5	21·5	27	25·5

MEN

	2007	2008	2009	2010	2011	2012	2013
At the gym	14	14	14.5	15	17	20	18
Jogging/running	5·5	7	6·5	6	6·5	8	7·5
Team sports	6	6·5	6·5	6·5	7	7	7·5
TOTAL	25·5	27·5	27·5	27·5	30·5	35	33

a) Draw a graph to support the statement: "On average men exercise for more hours a week than women."

b) Draw the graph that best illustrates the statement: "The gym is the most popular form of exercise for both men and women."

c) Draw the graph that best illustrates the statement: "The 2012 Olympic Games had a positive impact on the amount of exercise undertaken by men and women."

d) Draw two pie charts to illustrate the statement: "The average amount of time that women exercised in 2008 and 2011 was similar, but the time in the gym increased and the time spent jogging decreased."

1. Here is a drawing of a cuboid on isometric grid paper:

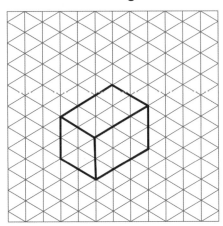

   On isometric paper, draw a cuboid that has a volume that is three times bigger than the one shown.

2. Each orange-shaded part of the circle is $\frac{1}{10}$ of the area of a circle.

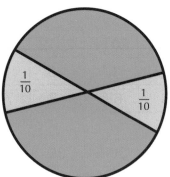

   What fraction of the circle is **one** of the blue areas? Give your answer in its lowest terms.

3. Here are three equations:

$m + n + r = 42$

$m + n = 17$

$n + r = 32$

Find the values of m, n and r.

4. In pattern 1, the ratio of blue squares to white squares is 5 : 3.

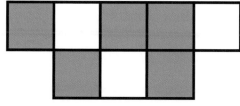

Pattern 1

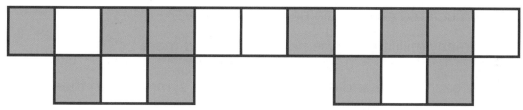

Pattern 2

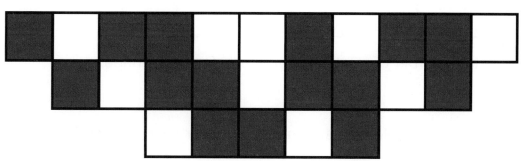

Pattern 3

a) What is the ratio of green squares to white squares in pattern 2?

b) What fraction of pattern 3 is white? Give your answer in its lowest terms.

5. The total cost of a new school building is £3 000 000. The cost breakdown is:

Materials: £2 000 000

Labour: £700 000

Other: £300 000

a) What fraction of the total cost is the labour? Give your answer in its simplest form.

b) What percentage of the total cost is the 'other' items?

6. Use trial and improvement to find the solution to $6r - r^2 = 7 \cdot 04$

7. A new colour of paint is made by mixing red, purple and yellow paint in the ratio 5 : 9 : 3. If 150 ml of yellow paint is used:

a) how much red and purple paint are required?

b) how many millilitres of the new paint would there be?

8. a) Copy each shape and draw all the lines of symmetry on these shapes.

b) Write the order of rotational symmetry for each shape.

9. $16 < 5h < 43$

Write all the possible whole number values for h which make this inequality true.

10. Simon wants to find out when his shop is busiest. He decides to count the number of customers in his shop at 2-hourly intervals for one day. Based on his observations, he concludes:

"My shop is busiest every day between 3 and 4."

a) Is he correct to draw this conclusion from his survey? Explain why.

b) Suggest two ways that he could improve his study.

11. Two boxes contain identical chocolates. The first box contains 24 chocolates and has a total mass of 108 g. The second box has a mass of 234 g.

a) Work out the mass of one chocolate.

b) How many chocolates are in the second box?

12. Three angles of a quadrilateral are 67°. Calculate the other angle.

13. Solve the equation $7(y + 5) + 3(16 - y) = 135$

14. A regular polygon has 8 sides.

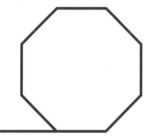

a) Work out the size of each exterior angle.

b) Use your answer to part (a) to work out the size of each interior angle.

15. A recipe for pasta sauce to serve 8 people is: 600 g tomatoes, 50 g basil and 20 g of butter.

   a) Write these quantities as a ratio of tomatoes : basil : butter.

   b) Write down an equivalent ratio to show the quantities of each ingredient to make this sauce for 2 people.

   c) What quantity of basil is needed to make this sauce for 4 people?

   d) How much butter is needed to make this sauce for 20 people?

16. The table shows the data collected in answer to the question "What is your favourite after-school activity?" The results have been given as percentages.

	Watching TV	Reading	Playing with friends	Art and craft activities	Shopping
Percentage who chose each option	45%	15%	30%	5%	5%

   a) Draw a pie chart to show this data. (Remember to convert the percentages to degrees – 100% = 360°.)

   b) What fraction chose shopping as their favourite after-school activity?

   c) Which is the most popular after-school activity?

   d) About what fraction chose watching TV or reading a book as their favourite after-school activity?

   e) About what fraction did not choose watching TV as their favourite after-school activity?

17. The nth term of a sequence (position-to-term rule) is $3(5n - 1)$

   a) Use the nth term to write the first five terms of the sequence.

   b) Write the term-to-term rule for the sequence.

   c) Work out the 17th term of the sequence.

18. $\dfrac{6}{12} + \dfrac{2}{8} = \dfrac{8}{20}$

What is wrong with this? Explain your answer fully and write the correct answer to the calculation.

19. Here is a trapezium:

    a) What is the size of angle a?

    b) Using the information you have been given
       and your answer to part (a), draw this
       trapezium in your book carefully. You can choose the length of your
       sides.

    c) Divide your trapezium into 2 identical right-angled triangles and
       1 rectangle. Mark on all lengths and angles.

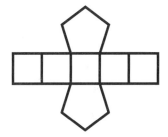

20. The 3rd, 4th and 5th terms of a sequence are:

    ___, ___, 60, 54·5, 49

    a) What is the term-to-term rule of the sequence?

    b) Write the first two terms of the sequence.

    c) What is the nth term of the sequence?

    d) Use your answer to part (c) to find the 48th term of the sequence.

21. Here is a net for a 3D shape.

    a) Name the 3D shape.

    b) How many edges, vertices and faces does
       the 3D shape have?

    c) If two of these 3D shapes were put together
       on a pentagonal face, how many faces would
       be visible on the final shape?

22. 145 children at Ellington School passed their end-of-year examinations in 2013. This increased to 190 in 2014. What was the percentage increase from 2013 to 2014? Give your answer to the nearest whole percentage.

23. Ella asked some people if they buy their groceries in store, online or both. The bar chart shows some of the results.

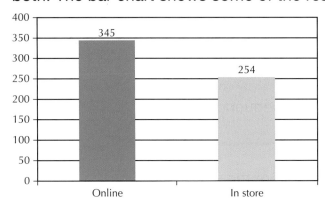

Altogether Ella surveyed 408 people. How many people shop **both** online and in store for their groceries?

24. $\dfrac{7}{9} - \dfrac{1}{3} = \dfrac{6}{6}$

What is wrong with this? Explain your answer fully and write the correct answer to the calculation.

25. a) Copy and complete the table of values for $y = 6x - 2$

x	−5	−1	1	3		7	
y	−32				34	40	52

b) Draw the graph of $y = 6x - 2$. Don't forget to choose an appropriate scale and label your axes.

26. The line graph shows the total number of animals in a zoo over a nine-year period.

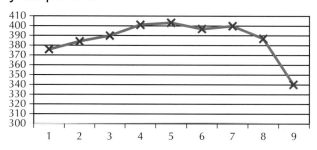

a) Suggest suitable labels for the x and y axes.

b) What type of data has been collected?

c) What could you say about the zoo between years 7 and 9?

d) What was the increase in number of animals between years 1 and 4?

27. Complete these calculations. Give your answers as proper fractions or mixed numbers.

a) $7 \times \dfrac{6}{12}$

b) $16 \div \dfrac{9}{10}$

c) $4 \times \dfrac{13}{15}$

d) $15 \div \dfrac{2}{5}$

Answers to review of learning questions

1. Correctly drawn cuboid with a volume of 36 cm³, e.g. $3 \times 2 \times 6$, $6 \times 1 \times 6$

2. $\dfrac{2}{5}$

3. $m = 10$; $n = 7$; $r = 25$

4. a) 10 : 7   b) $\dfrac{2}{5}$

5. a) $\dfrac{7}{30}$ b) 10%

6. $r = 1 \cdot 6$ or $4 \cdot 4$ (either answer is correct)

7. a) 250 ml red, 450 ml purple   b) 850 ml

8. a)

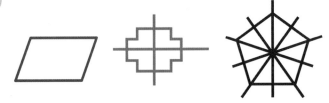

    b) parallelogram: 2   cross: 2   pentagon: 5

9. 4, 5, 6, 7 and 8

10. a) No. The survey was only for one day; the time intervals are quite big; his conclusion states between 3 and 4 when he only measured every two hours.

    b) He could do the survey each day for a month, consider the time of year; he could count the customers every 30 minutes rather than every two hours.

11. a) 4·5 g   b) 52

12. 159°

13. $y = 13$

14. a) 135°   b) 45°

15. a) 600 : 50 : 20   b) 150 : 12·5 : 5   c) 25 g   d) 50 g

16. a)

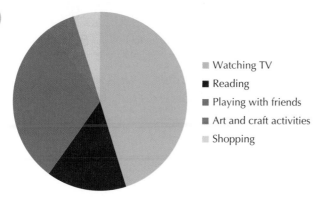

- Watching TV
- Reading
- Playing with friends
- Art and craft activities
- Shopping

b) $\dfrac{1}{20}$ c) Watching TV

d) $\dfrac{3}{5}$ e) Just over half $\left(\dfrac{11}{20}\right)$

17. a) 12, 27, 42, 57, 72   b) add 15   c) 252

18. The numerator and denominator have been added together instead of finding a common denominator. The correct calculation is: $\dfrac{6}{12} + \dfrac{2}{8} = \dfrac{12}{24} + \dfrac{6}{24} = \dfrac{18}{24} = \dfrac{3}{4}$

19. a) 72°   b) Check angles and lengths in drawings

20. a) take away 5·5   b) 1st term: 71   2nd term: 65·5
    c) $-5\cdot5n + 76\cdot5$ d) $-187\cdot5$

21. a) pentagonal prism   b) 7 faces, 15 edges, 10 vertices
    c) 7 faces

22. 31%

23. 191

24. The numerator and denominator have been subtracted from one another instead of finding a common denominator. The correct calculation is: $\dfrac{7}{9} - \dfrac{1}{3} = \dfrac{7}{9} - \dfrac{3}{9} = \dfrac{4}{9}$

25. a)

x	−5	−1	1	3	6	7	9
y	−32	−8	4	16	34	40	52

b)

26. a) x = years; y = number of animals in the zoo

b) discrete data over a time period (time series data)

c) the number of animals at the zoo declined

d) 25 animals

27. a) $3\frac{1}{2}$ **b)** $17\frac{7}{9}$ **c)** $3\frac{7}{15}$ **d)** $37\frac{1}{2}$